THEY CAME FROM BLAIR COUNTY
VOLUME 2

Eric Shields

THEY CAME FROM BLAIR COUNTY
VOLUME 2

Copyright © 2021 by Eric Shields

Printed and Electronic Versions
ISBN: 978-1-956353-03-7
(Eric Shields /Motivation Champs)

Cover Photo - Photographer unknown, photo provided by The Wolf Family

The book was printed
in the United States of America.

To order additional copies or bulk order contact the publisher, Motivation Champs Publishing. www.motivationchamps.com

DISCLAIMER

Dear Reader, the interviews that were conducted with the subjects for this book were conducted between July 2020 and August 2021. They reflect the lives and careers of the interviewees up until the time of their interview. However, due to many of the subjects still being very active in their careers, they may have experienced changes, major or minor, to their careers or lives since being interviewed that may not be mentioned in this book. For a complete update on their careers, please follow our subjects on their respective websites and social media.

CONTENTS

FOREWORD

Do you remember those career surveys teachers made you complete in high school? I always found myself selecting items in every single category. After adding up all my "points", my top three careers were listed right in front of me. All I had to do was fill out a sheet of paper! If only life was that simple. Yes, performing arts was listed as my top result, but I wanted to do it all! I still have dreams of being a safari guide, animal behaviorist, forensic analyst, and working for the CIA.

From my early years, the only thing I'd ever known was being on stage. My mother, Jackie Russo, who is featured in this book, owned and operated her own baton and dance studio. I spent countless nights there after school and knew I wanted to be a famous performer (or a veterinarian, but turns out, I'm too emotional).

I had spent so much time in performance related activities. I still thought I was meant to pursue a career in performing arts. After my wonderful mom and dad agreed to let me move to New York City after high school to attend an arts conservatory, something in my gut told me this was not my life's purpose. Deep down I knew I was meant to achieve fame in a more valuable way. I returned home to enroll in a fine arts program while soul searching for life's true meaning. I would find my own fame on my own terms and in my own way.

Fame is defined as the state of being known or talked about by many people, especially on account of notable achievements. Not everyone in the universe has to know your name to be famous! As someone who gets recognized by strangers on a daily basis from my segment of Typh's Picks on the local TV show All About Town, magazine print editorials, performing, and activism efforts. I finally understand this. It only took me thirty years to figure out that fame is fame no matter the scale.

The definition of fame does not include the words "celebrity", "Broadway star", or "multi-millionaire". The pressures of social media often fool people into believing their lives mean nothing unless they have thousands of followers or live in a big city. I could have easily given up everything and pursued a career in something that doesn't always guarantee success. Instead, I created my own definition of success and have found my own version of fame. I am a proud teacher, activist, performer, and world traveler who founded an organization "Bookworms Against Bullies".

I may not have reached global fame, but I know that I am admired by a lot of people in my community. For me, being an inspiration and positive role model to my students is what matters. I want to be known as the girl who used her talents to help make a difference in the lives of others.

I appreciate that Eric Shields thought me worthy enough to be included in volume one of this book and want to thank him for acknowledging the incredible people of Blair County.

—Typhani J. Russo

STEVE AUNGST

STEVE AUNGST

Steve Aungst was founder of the regional touring group The Vicksburg Quartet. He was founder and organizer of The Pennsylvania State Singing Convention which was held annually in Martinsburg, PA. If that wasn't enough, he was also a booking agent for local and regional music and variety acts as well as founder and director of The Meister Singers from Northern Bedford High School. Blair County native, Steve Aungst, said being in the music business has pretty much been his life.

Aungst grew up around Musselman's Grove in Claysburg. He saw some of the big acts that came in there, including The Sunshine Boys when he was about eight years old. He never got over that. He adds that he liked Gospel Music and liked country music. So, he developed The Vicksburg Quartet in 1965 or 1966.

In the early years, he says that The Vicksburgs performed all Gospel Music. In later years, they did a variety of good clean country music as well as Gospel. "We opened for a lot of the big stars of the time," Aungst explained.

Aungst's long-time friend and fellow quartet member, Jake Snyder, was the sound man and emcee. "We were together for over thirty years. We did a good many sound jobs for big stars."

Aungst, himself, did not sing. He was a classically trained

pianist. He graduated from Grace College in Winona Lake, Indiana and then did graduate work at Penn State. The Vicksburgs were also professionally trained and had music degrees, they sang in every state east of the Mississippi. They hosted trips to The Holy Lands, England and Scotland, taking thirty or forty people with them each time.

"We used to host tours which took us to fifteen different countries. We hosted cruises and bus trips and all types of stuff with the quartet," Aungst said.

The group mainly sang in Pennsylvania, West Virginia, Maryland, Ohio, and New York. Aungst says that they did those states quite a bit. He adds that there was a total of forty-two members of The Vicksburgs throughout the years. The ages of the members ranged from teenagers to guys in their forties and fifties. The youngest one started to play the drums with them when he was in eighth grade. "They saw that it wasn't so glamorous after a while. The life you had to live to do what we were doing."

Aungst added, "I was teaching school plus sometimes singing two hundred days a year. We were really pounding away. We had three tour buses. So, we had to hustle to pay for the buses. We sold a lot of records, and we had a lot of fans. We had a lot of popular places where we sang. We did everything that you could do except for hitting the big time."

They sang at The Wheeling Jamboree and the Lincoln

Jamboree in Kentucky. They also sang at a place called The Silver Mines. It was a big country music park in Lancaster, PA. There is no doubt about it, they sang in some big venues with some big stars.

Aungst organized The Pennsylvania State Singing Convention for forty years held annually in Martinsburg, PA with the last one being held in 2015. He was led by a desire to get the Gospel out to a fallen people.

They established their audience by partnering with a local radio station, which was Gospel radio station, WJSM and they knew them and got the word out about the PSSC. Also, the Vicksburgs were well known in the area, so they advertised the Gospel Sing. "We were totally amazed at how many people showed up for the first event."

Martinsburg was chosen as the site of the event because of its closeness to the home of The Vicksburg Quartet, about six miles away. The Morrison's Cove Memorial Park had a campground, a swimming pool, bowling alley and an old roller-skating rink, which is where the first PSSC was held. The first year, it rained "cats and dogs" and so they had many extra people in the roller-skating rink. The fire and police departments came and the wires were actually smoking and the lights were flickering. "I didn't think that roller skating rink ever had that much action. We managed to get the people out. We might have still had it inside the roller-skating rink another year, but then we moved it outside."

For several years, just about anybody who sang Gospel Music sang in Martinsburg. "We let anybody sing who wanted to sing as long as it was Gospel Music. A solo singer would get one song, a duet would get two, a trio would get three songs and a group might get four songs. That went on like that for a long time." They would have all kinds of Gospel music including Bluegrass, Southern Gospel, Black Gospel, and Contemporary. Though Contemporary was not the thing for Martinsburg, they still had it.

After a while, attendance started to die off a little, so they brought in the big names. They had everybody in from The Blackwood Brothers to The Chuck Wagon Gang to the Blue Ridge Quartet, Jeff and Sherry Easter, Gold City, and The Inspirations.

Aungst explained, "We still had all of the other people who wanted to sing and we let them sing. Then, at eight o'clock at night, we would bring up the big group and let them sing for an hour. That really brought in the audience."

It came to an end in 2015, after forty years. "I just got tired. I couldn't do it anymore. I was getting older. I was worn out," Aungst added. "We had a lot of people who liked it and volunteered. We had about forty people who would volunteer year after year after year."

They had people come every year from Canada. They would come from Florida to see the Gospel Sing. On a Friday or Saturday night it would attract around 2,500 people. The largest single day crowd was around three to four thousand people.

Aungst says a lot of people got saved by hearing the Gospel through music. Every Sunday morning, he says they had a fundamental church service. "We would always have a group, who could not only sing, but could also preach, like The Couriers, for example. A lot of people were saved, and a lot of lives were changed. People would come back thirty years, later and would share how the PSSC made a difference in their lives.

Aungst also promoted Gospel sings at Knoebel's Amusement Park and Landisville Campground in Pennsylvania and Cumberland Fairgrounds in Cumberland, MD.

In addition to the quartet and the Gospel Sing, there was The Meister Singers. Aungst taught school at Northern Bedford High School. He had taught music and directed the senior high chorus. Then, he had formed a show group called The Meister Singers. He had thirty-four different versions of them. They became very popular. There were times that they were singing seventy days a year. They sang in Maryland, Pennsylvania, and West Virginia. There were nine kids in the group because that was how many you were allowed to haul in the van. Their shows were choreographed. They would sing and dance. They would be dressed up. They looked like a million bucks, and they sounded good, too.

Years ago, the quartet would play the fairs and they would attend the Pennsylvania State Fair Convention, which was always in January. They would do a showcase and they would get up and do their thing for about twenty minutes in front of the people who were buying talent for fairs. "That is how we got so many fairs and got the agents. There were about six or eight different agents across the country who wanted to showcase us."

A group called The Sunshine Express and another group called Life. There were these singing groups of young people, which were young adults in their twenties. They were groups, who would open for acts such as Bob Hope. "That is where I got the idea for this high school group. I patterned them after these groups. They sang for anything that you could imagine…Potentate's reception to the Lions club to dog shows…anything that you could think of"

They would sing a variety of music including a lot of big band stuff. Each member would do a solo, either a country solo or a Broadway solo. "I tried to help them develop what they were best at, then I would give them songs to sing that they could shine at."

Aungst also had a booking agency, where he would book entertainment. He would book just about everybody in the area including The Fabulous Flashbacks and Dan & Galla. People would call him to book entertainment for all types of events.

The Vicksburgs recorded forty albums in studios in places such as Greenville, SC, Mechanicsburg, PA, and Nashville.

Steve Aungst was inducted into The Pennsylvania Southern Gospel Music Association Hall of Fame in 2004.

**Information for this article was obtained through an in-person interview with Steve Aungst
**Photos were provided by Steve Aungst

GREGG BRANDT

GREGG BRANDT

Raised in the Garden Heights section of Altoona, Gregg Brandt went to Carnegie Mellon University for musical theatre and vocal performance and graduated in 1989. He attributes his success in life to some really good teachers who took their time and said, "You're really talented. Maybe you might want to consider going into this field."

Brandt's parents were really supportive. They knew about the arts, but they just sang in church. "Singing in church is pretty much how I got started. I'm thankful for such supportive and loving parents."

While at Carnegie Mellon, Brandt auditioned for things like The Pittsburgh Civic Light Opera and The Pittsburgh Opera. After performing many productions with each arts organization, he adds that one thing leads to another and ended up doing a couple of national tours.

He was still doing some things on the side while working on his master's degree at Carnegie Mellon University. Brandt ended up not finishing it because he got some other shows, including a national tour. He ended up being a couple of classes short.

Brandt was cast in the Broadway production of *Les Misérables* in October 1996. He debuted on November 1, 1996. "I was part of their tenth anniversary vision, which was March 12, 1997. I was part of the new regime, in a way."

He stayed with the show until January 2003. He and his son became the first father/son team to perform the show together. "My son was seven, almost eight. He actually just finished performing in the Broadway revival production of *Annie Get Your Gun* starring Reba McEntire. They asked if I would be willing to go perform on the national tour with my son and I jumped at the opportunity. I was what they called a 'Swing', which meant I understudied all the roles in the show except for a couple of the lead characters and I would go on in a moment's notice. I was also the Dance Captain which was kind of like an assistant director for that kind of show because there was not a lot of dancing. That is how I got interested in directing more."

Brandt later returned to the Broadway Company for two more years before leaving the show in 2003. That's when he began teaching and moved back to Altoona. His son and daughter went to elementary school there and Roosevelt Junior High before it was torn down. "I think my son was one of the last classes through Roosevelt."

Brandt was also an adjunct professor at various local colleges in Altoona and in Pittsburgh. He also finished his remaining courses for his master's degree at Carnegie Mellon University.

He was later cast in the original musical, *A Tale of Two Cities* in 2008. He explains that, unfortunately, some shows like Les Mis last so long for an actor and that is awesome. It lasted five or six years. However, he was only in *A Tale of*

Two Cities for two months. The whole financial crisis had a crippling effect on new as well as some existing Broadway productions.

Brandt accepted a position as a musical theater voice and acting professor at Rider University in New Jersey. His son ended up going to college there because he had the performance bug as well. He continued to teach at Rider University as well as NYU (Tisch) in New York City.

He has been teaching and directing at Saint Vincent College in Latrobe since December 2014. He has directed over twenty-five musicals and plays during his tenure there. "I love New York City. I am hoping to possibly retire there and continue directing or casting for productions after all is said and done at St Vincent," Brandt said.

He explained that St Vincent is the best of both worlds. Academically, he is the only theatre professor and directs the fall play as well as the spring musical. Then, he casts and directs the professional summer theatre season where he is the Producing Artistic Director. "I am only the fourth director in the fifty-two-year history of the prestigious Saint Vincent Summer Theatre."

Brandt still performs and sings in Broadway-style concerts. He loves to sing with orchestras or do Broadway Revues. He still sings in church, too. "It's nice to be a church soloist. It keeps me singing and connected. It makes my soul feel complete."

Brandt recalls that when he got the call to be in the Broadway production of *Les Misérables*, he was living in the Pittsburgh area and traveling to New York in between work to audition. At the time, in addition to getting call backs for *Les Misérables*, he was also getting called back for Miss Saigon. Both were controlled by the same casting agency, Johnson-Liff Casting. They controlled a lot of the big newer shows such as *Phantom of the Opera*, *Les Misérables*, *Cats*, and *Miss Saigon*.

When he finally got the call, he thought that it was going to be for *Miss Saigon*. However, it turned out to be for Les Mis. Brandt explained that "Back when I was in college, Les Mis had just opened, and everybody wanted to be in it. It was the show every young performer aspired to be in."

He was teaching some private voice lessons at a church and when he arrived home, he was informed he missed a call from the casting agency. Once he got the official offer, he says that it felt so surreal, "like is this really happening?" Brandt explained, "It was a Friday afternoon and I had to be in New York City by Monday afternoon. I had my whole life turned upside down."

He stayed on a friend's couch for about six weeks until he found a studio apartment on the Upper West Side. He says it was a dream come true, especially with that show. He adds that it was definitely worth all of the trips to New York, driving so much just to go up and sing sixteen or thirty-two measures of a song.

He left the show in January 2003 and the show closed later that year in May. He went back for two weeks in March to fill in because he knew all of the roles. One of the understudies got sick and someone else was out due to an injury. "They asked me to come in and perform a specific role for two weeks."

Brandt also did a National Tour of *Camelot* starring Stacy Keach as King Arthur for about four months. Brandt also did a tour of *Bells Are Ringing*, which was out of Goodspeed Opera House in Connecticut. He was in Grad School at the time. That is why he left. The music director at Pgh CLO, who was music directing that show. He called and said, "We just lost one of our guys and this would be perfect for you. Drop what you are doing and come up, because after Goodspeed, we will be going on tour for six months."

Brandt recalls, "It is funny looking back on it and that was back in 1991 and people like Rob Ashford, Andy Blankenbuehler and Casey Nicholaw, all of these Broadway director names now, were in shows with me. They were in the ensemble, like supporting role kind of thing. Now, they are all major directors and choreographers on Broadway. They are friends of mine. I don't talk to them very often, but I saw Rob when I was in New York last year. Theater friends are all like family."

Brandt says that being on tour saves some money, because they pay for your expenses and your hotel room, and they give you some sort of per diem. "It is a paid trip to see the United States!"

The Les Mis tour went everywhere. He and his son were out there for a year. The other tours weren't as long. "When we were on the Les Mis tour, we were everywhere. In fact, I drove a lot of places because Eddie, my son, was tutored by the Wrangler, an adult, certified teacher and somewhat of a babysitter too. So, I had to drive because Eddie had to be down at the theater for classes." He adds that it was nice because then, they could sight-see and do things rather than be stuck in a hotel sometimes. Their biggest trip was going from Ontario to Dallas, TX in two days. "It was a lot but that is what memories are made of."

He says that he still has a photo album from whenever they were on tour. They got a card from every city that they went to with the hotel information and the theater information. He adds that he kept all of these things and additional mementos. "It is crazy how time flies because my son is almost twenty-eight now."

Brandt says that the initial spark for him started in church…singing hymns in the pew with his family. His parents asked him if he would like to sing in the choir. They could tell that he could sing. He agreed and one thing led to another and as they say, the rest is history.

Then, in elementary school, he was singing in the all-city chorus and then in junior high, he was in the musicals and various concerts. "There were some teachers who told me that you should look into doing this more."

He always had that fun personality and got along with others, and he had some good teachers in both junior and senior high school. "One show leads to another and then I was getting leads. It just sort of stuck with me."

As far as singing with symphonies and orchestras, he recently performed a concert in Doylestown. A friend of his who worked with him on *Amazing Grace, the Musical* (Brandt directed the initial readings and concert performances) teaches at a high school there and they had a Broadway night.

He also sang with The New Jersey Festival Orchestra on

New Year's Eve a couple of years ago. They bring in different artists and they sing with a forty to fifty-piece orchestra. Brandt says there's nothing quite like performing with a live orchestra and creating beautiful music together.

Brandt fondly recalls growing up in Altoona. He says that the arts are really strong there. Altoona Community Theatre is wonderful and there are a lot of great teachers for music, theater, and dance. "I was fortunate at the time. I believe a lot in being blessed with the opportunities. I am a pretty religious person, but you also need a little luck along the way too."

He was fortunate enough to live in the same household where his parents stayed together. Brandt adds, "There wasn't social media and all of these distractions. That could be good or bad. I think for me at the time, it was good. I was able to focus on the things that I needed to that made me prepare as an artist." He says that he was blessed to get where he is in both his personal life and career. You must work hard, too and your talent has to be there.

"Without those teachers and super supportive parents, I don't think that I would have been able to pursue a career in the performing arts. I don't think that I would have gone as far as I did and have a career in it. I simply don't think that would have happened."

The advice that he would offer to those who have big goals is to never give up. If you love, eat, sleep, and drink performing in the arts whether they play an instrument or dance, no matter what their passion is, they have to go for it. He says that this day and age, there are so many talented people and with the internet helping to get them out there and getting them noticed, they have to do anything and everything that they can. "They have got to keep doing what they are blessed with and doing what they feel like they have been put on this earth to do. Don't give up. There are always things or people that may hold you back, but if it is something you feel you need to do, then, by all mean, pursue your dreams. You have to have that drive and passion to want to succeed."

**Information for this article was obtained through a phone interview with Gregg Brandt
**Photos were taken and copywritten by Photographer Brian Ray Norris

DAVE BURKET AND BURKET FALLS FARM

John and Dave Burket from Burket Falls Farm

DAVE BURKET AND BURKET FALLS FARM

In the rural area of Blair County, known as Greenfield Township, in a section known as Pole Cat Hollow, is Burket Falls Farm. This farm is known world-wide for the registered Holstein dairy cattle with the polled (naturally hornless) and red hair coat genes that they have developed and bred. Today, over two-thirds of all polled Holsteins in the world trace their roots to Burket Falls Farm.

The farm was established in 1928 by Frank W. Burket. His son, Dave, assumed responsibility of the family farm at the age of fourteen when his father was injured and unable to work the farm. "Dad was going to sell the farm. I talked him out of it. Since I was only fourteen, I was still in school. I got up early and worked before school and went back to work after school," Dave remembers.

Dave's son, John, currently runs the farm. He said that when his dad took over the dairy farm, they had mostly Guernsey and Crossbreeds. Then, in 1960, he says that his dad decided that he wanted some registered Holsteins. So, Dave went with a friend to Wisconsin and purchased a group of registered Holsteins. Dave says that there were twenty-two cows in a trailer. His friend bought eleven and he, himself, bought eleven.

Dave recalls, "It just so happened that one of the cows that I bought had a calf, which never developed horns." He remembers that the only thing that was different about that calf was that she was such an aggressive eater. She would eat anything that the older cattle would eat. He says, "That is unusual. Usually, all they want is milk."

She didn't grow any horns but there wasn't much thought about it. However, she produced at about twice the herd average with really high butter fat.

Dairy cows, for the most part, are all born with horns. John says that they don't have horns when they are born, but genetically they have them and the older they get, the more they grow. They can become an issue in working with them with people as well as other animals.

Dave adds that there is no humane way to dehorn calves. "If the animal rights people would see you burning the horns off of a calf, they would want to put you in jail. It is cruel."

Dave began to take notice and he began to inquire about the polled gene. He knew nothing about it. "I didn't know it was dominant." He adds, "That got us to pay attention."

Dave sought the advice of the better cowmen in the nation. He continues that the system that they had didn't always agree with the mavericks. He believed in good cattle and the system at the time was all on index on numbers. If a cow had numbers, she was a good cow by their standards. "To me if a cow was a good cow, a good-looking cow and produced a lot of milk, it was a good cow to me."

There were a lot of people who understood the advantage of the polled gene. John explains that it is the gene that dad lucked into. He adds that fortunately for him, this animal that never developed horns was the best cow that he had in his herd. She was an extremely high producer and set several national records in milk production back in the 60s and 70s.

John continues, "Dad always had a vision of this genetically polled gene becoming a value." It was that gene that he worked with and capitalized on and today the polled gene is sought after because there is not a nice way to take horns off of cattle. You either have to burn them off electronically or you have to surgically remove them. It is all painful to the animal. You have got to give the animal anesthesia. You have to have a veterinarian on site. To circumvent all of that, he has bred them genetically hornless. The demand for polled cattle around the world over the last twenty-five years has grown immensely.

John also says that in the early days, the naysayers laughed at him, thinking it was all a foolish idea. But John said his dad never let that bother him. He just continued on. He has been recognized in the state, the country and around the world as a pioneer in polled Holstein breeding.

Dave and the farm have been inducted into The Pennsylvania Holstein Hall of Fame back in 2003. This is quite a prestigious honor. He was inducted into The National Dairy Shrine in 2018 which is an honor that they give around the world. They recognized him as a pioneer in Dairy Cow Breeding as recently as October 2018. About two years ago, Holstein International, a magazine published in about ten different languages and is published around the world, recognized him as one of the most influential Holstein breeders in the last twenty-five years. The farm also won the ACE Award, which is The Blair County Agriculture Excellence Award, given by The Blair County Chamber of Commerce to recognize someone in agriculture. He has also received recognition from his local area when he was inducted into the Claysburg Hall of Fame in July 2021.

Dave and Betty Burket

John says that his dad is quite a humble guy. He doesn't bask in the limelight, but he feels that he has been vindicated in the pursuit of his dream, which is to breed the dairy cow polled or hornless. He always made the comment that someday the Holstein breed would be polled. That is, slowly but surely coming to fruition, primarily based on his work.

As far as being inducted into the Claysburg Hall of Fame, Dave says that he feels honored to be recognized by his neighbors and people in this immediate area. He always said that people away from here knew what they were doing at the farm, including people across the state, across the country and across the world. However, he says that he is not sure that their neighbors knew what was happening there, as far as their success in breeding Holsteins.

He got state awards. He got recognition from the state as well as on a national level, but the people closest to them probably were the last to realize what all he had accomplished in his eighty-nine years.

Dave says that he really is not surprised at the attention his farm has received because of the good sound cows that they had and the fact that they were naturally polled. "I figured that it would catch on and it has. I don't know that I realized that it would be to the extent that it is today. The breed will be polled in time."

Dave remembers growing up in Claysburg fondly. "I had some good people behind me. My grandpap was probably the most respected person in the community. People went to him for advice. Dad had a good mind, but he was crippled. I had a good family. Now, John has been calling the shots for the last thirty-five years."

There isn't a lot of people who don't know what we are doing, but the people who do know encourage him and support him to carry on. John adds, "Dad always told us, 'Don't throw the polled gene away.' If something were to happen to him, keep the polled gene at the forefront of what your goals are."

John continues that he doesn't think that his dad ever thought that he would become world famous over this, but he thought his dad always felt that for the betterment of mankind and animal kind that the polled gene would be something noteworthy and go down in history as a noble cause.

Both Dave and John say that if you go to Europe or if you go to Australia and speak to dairymen and ask them about the polled Holstein gene, they will recognize Burket Falls Farm as being its source. The whole family has been fortunate enough to travel extensively, but it is refreshing to go to another country where they can't even speak your language and they know you because of what you accomplished in the dairy industry.

John also says that he should credit his mother some, as well. He says that she worked alongside his dad. They have been married for sixty-nine years. She supported him and his endeavors 100%. When they had international visitors, she helped host them. She cooked for them and provided for them. She was kind of a key cog in the success of the farm.

"As a result of the accomplishments that my father made

here on the farm, we have had literally thousands of visitors over the years. They have come from all fifty states, forty countries and six continents. In doing all of that, it took a lot of work and preparation to prepare for visitors and so forth. My mother was always by his side in every way," John adds.

John says that with visitors coming from places like Japan, Hungary, Australia, and Italy, that in their little community, there has probably never been a location where there has been as much international activity as there is here on this little farm in Polecat Hollow.

He adds, "Our genetics have been spread in every state that there is dairy cattle as well as countries around the world." The impact of that is far reaching.

Addressing the future, John says that their plans are to continue in the dairy business and to continue marketing genetics like we have over the past fifty years. "We supplement our milk income with the work of genetics. That is our plan going forward. I am the third generation, the fourth generation is my children. They are all in on it."

As far as the legacy of the farm, John says that he is just awfully proud of the hard work that his parents put into making the farm what it is. He says that his role is kind of a small one. He feels blessed to step into the management role and to continue on the tradition.

John says that people laughed at them and made fun

of them because of what they were trying to do. "It never caused us to pause or discontinue what we were doing." He continues, "Dad always said that what we are doing is the right thing to do. We have never deviated from that philosophy. The naysayers were big. We were kind of swimming up stream against the system because the system that was in place wasn't necessarily condoning the type of cattle that we were breeding. We have proved the system wrong. It took us fifty years, but it is kind of sweet revenge."

Sophia the Cow, the prized Holstein that made Burket Falls Farm World famous

Sophia the cow, one of the cows that made the farm known, was born in 1974. She was selected in 2013 as one of the seven most impactful Holsteins ever bred or developed in the state of Pennsylvania. This recognition was made during the centennial celebration of the Pennsylvania Holstein Association.

The two cows that primarily made the farm known are buried in their yard.

As far as advice goes, Dave says that, if they are pursuing something that is advantageous to mankind, you can live here or you can live anywhere else. You don't have to live in a metropolitan area.

John says that you have to stay focused and stay true to your roots. "I do believe that anything that one sets out to do, they are able to accomplish it. My father proved that. I am fifty-seven years old and I watched all of those years. My father stayed true to his principles. He never deviated from what he felt was the right thing to do and doing it the right way. It was a tremendous lesson for anyone, particularly his children, his three sons, watching him and how he worked. He worked extremely hard, but he was never intimidated by what the neighbors and the naysayers were doing. He stayed focused and stayed true to his roots. He has been a tremendous success within the dairy industry, not only locally but around the world."

**Information for this article was obtained through in-person interviews with John and Dave Burket

**Photos were supplied by John and Dave Burket

GENE DECKER

GENE DECKER

Blair County native Gene Decker started to play baseball in the Blair Twilight League. A man from Altoona came out to see him play in Woodbury. He ended up signing him up for an Altoona team in the City League. That was followed by getting involved with a team from Six Mile Run. "While I was playing for that league, a guy from Everett came out to see me play. That's how I got involved with the Pen-Mar League."

The Pen-Mar League was a semi-pro league which consisted of teams from Pennsylvania, Maryland, and West Virginia. "I started to play in that league in 1971. The guy, who got me involved with that league was Richard Crawford. We became very good friends." Decker ended up playing with and against a lot of guys who had made the pros. They included Johnny Kruk, who was with the Phillies.

In 1995, a guy by the name of Joey Piotti got a team together to go down to Florida. It was called the Roy Hobbs Tournament. It was made up of guys forty and over. "At the time, I think that I was either fifty-eight or fifty-nine. I played in that and was seen down there by a lot of guys. I played with them up until I quit in 2015." He continues, "I played with them for twenty years, going to Florida, Phoenix, Vegas and all over the place to play ball."

There were a lot of former pros in that league as well. "A teammate of mine was Ron LeFlore and I played against

Bill Lee, who had pitched for the Red Sox, and Bert Campanaris." No one could believe that I never had a sore arm. "I could pitch two days in a row."

Decker can't explain his love of the game. He says that he just loves baseball.

He explains, "My dad played. When I was only about ten years old, my dad built me a mound. 60ft 6in. Not a little league distance. When he would get off the work bus, he would go in the house. In those days supper was ready at five o'clock. He would sit there and drink his cup of coffee. When he was done, he would come out and I would throw to him from the time he would finish his coffee until five o'clock when supper was ready."

He continues, "I really looked forward to that. In the field of Dreams, there is a line in there that says, 'I would never play catch, I would just like to play catch with my dad.' I miss him. I miss my father. He was good to me. He taught me a lot about baseball. I would raise hell with guys when they would have an error. He took me to the side one day and said, 'that guy who just had the error will probably be the guy who would get the base hit to drive in a runner to make you a winner.' He had a lot of knowledge."

Decker has fond memories of Blair County. "I grew up in McKee. The only time that I was out of Blair County was when I was in the service. When I came back, I met my wife. We lived here in Blair County. I can't say whether it helped or hindered my baseball career, because I never got any exposure other than Blair County."

He recalls, "If I was to pick out one game in my life that I would like to see over again. It was a no-hitter, but it wasn't because it was a no-hitter. The camaraderie of the ball players and they all came together and gelled that one game. Everybody picked up everybody. I still get goose bumps when I talk about that game. I know that when the last out was recorded, Jack Morgan was on first base. He threw the ball up in the air and they realized it was a no-hitter. I was sitting on the mound, and I was crying. I knew that I had a no-hitter. That was probably the best game that I ever played in. I can remember the game almost like it was yesterday and that was in 1972."

Decker has some great advice for those wanting to reach their goals. "You have got to have the three Ds. Determination, dedication, and desire. If you don't have the desire to play, you have got to get out. You have to work at the game. You have to refine your skills. Like me, I would throw with my dad." He continues, "Pitching became natural to me. I would work on specialty control. Everybody said that control was my worst enemy because I could put a baseball where I wanted when I was pitching."

Decker has received many trophies and awards throughout his long career. In 2011, he was inducted into the Broad Top Hall of Fame and in 2018 he was inducted into the Semi-Pro National Baseball Hall of Fame in Evansville, Indiana. He has also thrown a total of five no-hitters.

Gene has a lot of accomplishments and very fond memories, but the thing he cherishes the most is the friends and friendships that he has made over the years.

**Information for this article was obtained through an in-person interview with Gene Decker
**Photo was provided by Gene Decker

ANGELA DODSON DAEGER

ANGELA DODSON DAEGER

Her love for Johnny Cash has propelled Roaring Spring native Angela Dodson Daeger into a career that any die-hard fan of the man in black would envy.

It all started when she fell in love with music when she was eleven years old. She says that she always loved country. She grew up listening to Leann Rimes and Bryan White. Her parents took her to concerts including one at The Bryce Jordan Center in State College to see them play. "I just loved what they were doing."

Her grandparents also had an influence by raising her on Johnny Cash, Johnny Horton, Patsy Cline and Loretta Lynn.

She realized that she could sing at the age of eleven. Living in a small town, she tried to figure out outlets and ways to perform and get better and grow that talent. "I was really lucky that my family was very supportive. "

They went to an event at St Patricks in Newry where Dennie Huber was holding a karaoke night. She sang Leann Rimes' "One Way Ticket" and "Blue". Dennie helped get her started. "He opened things up for me and introduced me as the pride of Roaring Spring, Pennsylvania. That made me so happy and so proud." He helped her gain confidence and helped her play at several places, including Crazyfest.

As she got older, she continued playing shows anywhere and everywhere around town which allowed her to get to know people.

She says that she also got to know Jack Servello and went into the studio with him and recorded a couple of tracks, so she could have a CD to sell at her shows. She also worked with Steve Aungst, who, she says, "was amazing." He put her on a circuit, where they would go from town to town, playing community events and for nursing homes.

Wanting to sing as much as possible, Angela performed many benefits including Toys for Tots, Make-a-Wish and Relay for Life events, and even some unique places like grocery stores and gun shows! She said that she even sang at a motorcycle rally where you couldn't hear her because they were revving so loud. "I was still just happy to have a place to play."

She studied at Mount Aloysius, where she attended from 2005 until 2009. During this time, she joined a band called The Country Outlaws. They toured around Altoona, Huntingdon, Bellefonte, Mt Union, and all throughout PA. "We were like weekend warriors with our music."

In 2009, the band decided to go their separate ways and Angela graduated from college. That was when she realized that this was her opportunity to move to Nashville, which was a huge step for her. "My mom thought it was far when I moved thirty minutes away to school. Now I was moving over ten hours away!"

She says that she always had a great love for Johnny Cash.

"He really resonated with me. I think that it was the authenticity that he had. When he sang something, it was believable. Every note might not always be absolutely perfect, but whatever words he sang, you believed it." She adds that, as a songwriter, she could really relate to him.

When she moved to Nashville, she played on Broadway. She played a lot of shows and got to know the people there.

In PA, she had always been told that she could either be a big fish in a small pond or a little fish in a big ocean. That is definitely what it felt like for her to come to Nashville. She says it was exciting to be around people who shared that interest and love and were musicians who got it. However, she adds, that it was also overwhelming because she wasn't really that special anymore because she was doing what everybody else was doing. It was a little bit harder to carve her own niche. She worked at a preschool during the day just to make some money and at night she was playing honky tonks.

With her focus still on her love for Johnny Cash along with rockabilly and classic country, she wrote the song "They Called Him Cash". One day, she came across John Carter Cash's email online. She didn't know if it was real, but she decided to give it a shot. They had a studio called The Cash Cabin Studio. It was a cabin that Johnny had in the 1970s in the woods on his property. Later in life, when Johnny was starting to get ill, he changed it into a studio. That way he could work from home and not have to travel.

They were still operating it as a studio. Angela sent the song to John Carter and thought that she maybe could record the song and see what would happen.

It wasn't until she had played until two in the morning the night before and then woke up at six to go to her pre-school job that she received a call from John Carter. He said he heard her song and he really liked it and wanted her to come into the studio and record it. She was thrilled!

Recording a five song EP correctly with the recording, the best musicians, and the best artwork was not cheap. This was 2013 and Kickstarter was big at the time. So, she started a Kickstarter campaign. The way it worked was if someone would donate money in advance, then once the CD comes out, donors would receive a CD plus some other promotional items. That is when the Cove came together. They wrote newspaper articles to announce the project. "My hometown came together, and they raised all of the money that I needed in order to do this project. It was absolutely amazing. They really pulled together. I could not have done it without them." That is how she was able to record her Johnny Cash song and some other originals at Cash Cabin.

This is also when she ended up with Icon Entertainment. She adds that 2013 was when The Johnny Cash Museum opened. All of a sudden, there was this place, where these people who loved Johnny Cash were starting this museum.

Icon Entertainment was started by Bill and Shannon Miller. Bill was close personal friends with Johnny for many years. That is what has always drawn her to the museum because it was truly formed out of love and respect from one friend to another. She says that you can tell that when you walk through the museum. She loved everything there. "I was there so much that I think eventually they just decided they should hire me!"

Now, she is Senior Vice President of the company. She handles the marketing, tourism, and public relations for each company under the Icon Entertainment Group umbrella. "It is amazing how my love for Johnny Cash has taken me in a totally different but equally amazing direction here in Nashville."

The Johnny Cash Museum is on the first floor. On the second floor is The Patsy Cline Museum. "Getting to know the Cash family and the Cline family has been great," she adds. "We have had events where we have the family come and perform." She says that she has also gotten to know Tommy Cash, too, and has performed with him many times. She has also performed Patsy Cline tribute shows with Patsy's daughter Julie Fudge in the audience. She says that experiences like that have been mind-blowing and amazing. "They are all down to earth and so sweet."

Icon's newest venture, Johnny Cash's Kitchen and Saloon is right next door to the museum. They have fried chicken and home cooking. Johnny loved Swett's restaurant, which is a Nashville staple. As a result, they brought Swett's recipes in, as well. Literally, you can eat Johnny's favorite food. They have recreated what some of the rooms in his house would look like. You can sit on a leather couch in front of a fire and eat his favorite fried chicken meal.

Angela says that she got to be part of the creative process when it came to the saloon. From when they were writing down initial ideas with what would be interestng to fill this building to being a part of picking out the photos that were going to hang on the wall, she was involved.

They also have two restaurants. There's Skull's Rainbow Room, which is a jazz spot located in Printers Alley. They have fine dining and craft cocktails. It has been a Nashville staple since 1948. Skull's hosted all of the greats back in the day and still has the same checkerboard stage where Johnny Cash, Waylon Jennings, Patsy Cline, and many others performed.

The newest business in their organization is House of Cards, which is in the basement of the Johnny Cash Museum. It's a speakeasy. They didn't do any signage. The idea is that you should hear about it from word of mouth. You walk into the museum, but you don't realize that there is anything there. Then, there is a security guard, who takes you down the secret tunnel to the basement. It is totally magic themed. It is also fine dining. It is the entire package, where magicians come to your table and perform high end magic tricks. It is a really cool experience. There is definitely nothing like it in Nashville.

They also have Nudie's Honky Tonk, which honors Nudie Cohn, who created the sparkling rhinestone suits seen at the Opry in the 1950's. He created items for Johnny Cash and Patsy Cline and for everyone from Elton John to John Wayne. The honky tonk has live music and food and drinks.

Angela and her husband Dave Daeger ended up meeting through the Johnny Cash connection. His story is very similar to hers. He grew up in a small town in Indiana, loved music and eventually moved to Nashville. He got hooked up with John Carter Cash, playing guitar, which has been amazing for him because he has since played the Grand Ole Opry, the Bridgestone Arena, the Ryman Auditorium and more. He has played with Loretta Lynn, Chris Cornell, Kris Kristofferson, Ronnie Dunn, Sheryl Crow, Jamey Johnson, and many others.

Angela first met him when she was working at The Johnny Cash Museum, where they were doing a birthday bash celebrating Johnny's birthday. Her future husband was there playing guitar with John Carter. Angela and Dave had both separately recorded at the cabin and were at the cabin together to practice shows that they have done.

As soon as they were engaged, they just knew that since both Johnny and the cabin were so important to them, that is where they wanted to get married. John Carter is just like a brother to Dave. They decided to ask him to officiate. Angela says that by this time it was a natural fit. She adds, "We kept our wedding pretty small. I don't think we even had thirty people there. We just had it out on the property. It was a beautiful day."

Angela and Dave performing at their wedding.

As far as the future goes, she says she absolutely loves working for Icon. She is going to keep going with that and see what the future holds. Icon's next venture is going to be with The Frank Sinatra Estate. They will be bringing something like that to the Printers Alley area as well as continuing to promote and preserve the legacies of traditional county artists like Johnny Cash and Patsy Cline. With her music, Angela will continue to do videos and play shows with her husband. An upcoming project that she is excited about is a song she recently wrote and will soon be releasing featuring country singer Bryan White on guitar.

Angela fondly remembers growing up in a small town, explaining how you have a lot of time to sit and think and daydream and work on your skills. There is not always a ton of things to do, so you have to find ways to entertain yourself. "For me, that was songwriting and practicing the same songs until I drove my parents insane. It was actually good for honing a craft." She added that it was great to have people who support you and build you up. That was huge for her because her whole family was always very encouraging. That is what helped her to be brave enough to go and spread her wings.

The advice that she would offer to people, living in a small town, who would like to achieve their goals would be first to read this book because it is inspiring. She says that she wishes that she had a resource like this when she was a kid. She feels that it would have been something to inspire her to be able to say, "Look at all of these people who did this." A lot of it is finding whatever your passion is. It could be anything. You need to find that passion and not be afraid to go after it. You can feel when you are in a small town that the people and the support are there.

**Information for this article was obtained through a phone interview with Angela Dodson Daeger
**Photos were provided by Angela Dodson Daeger

JANET ELDRED

JANET ELDRED

Hollidaysburg library director Janet Eldred's courageous battle with early-onset dementia has helped to earn her a national award.

The American Library Association's Lemony Snicket Prize for Noble Librarians Facing Adversity was established in 2014 by the association in partnership with Daniel Handler. The prize, which is administered by ALA's Governance Office annually recognizes and honors a librarian who has faced adversity with integrity and dignity intact.

Winning this year's award was a thrill of a lifetime for Janet. "It was one of the top things that has happened over my lifetime," she says.

She adds that it simply acknowledges the work that she is able to do in spite of the mental ineptitude that she has right now. "I just do the best with what I have," Janet says. The Board of Directors have been very supportive as have the library patrons.

Janet's husband Keith says that they have been aware of the award for several years, now. Since they knew that they would be telling her story for medical challenges, anyway, they thought they may as well apply for this. He says that it was early 2021 that the deadline came. He held off until then because he felt that they needed to have some of their This is Red Project behind them and not just be an idea but something that they were following through on.

After they got through 2020, which of course the library had its challenges during the pandemic including the fact that at one time Janet was the only employee working. Everybody else was laid off. "While those challenges were going on, we planned to publish the twenty books for This is Red." He says that as they got toward the end of the year, he knew that he was going to complete those.

He explained that they have a story to back up her situation and that brought them to early Spring 2021. They applied for the award and crossed their fingers. But so much time passed. They kind of forgot about it, then Janet received an email. It so happens that the chair of the selection committee had tried to call both of their phones but missed both of them. They both saw the email at the same time. It was such a shot in the arm for Janet, because at different points, she would get very low and say, "Should I continue on? Is it the best thing for the library?" It was a huge validation for her to receive the award. They, also, were pleased with the fact that when their boys were little, Lemony Snicket, the book, The Series of Unfortunate Events books were important to their family, because they entertained their boys and they entertained themselves as well. On car trips, they would listen to the audio books. It was a very pleasing closing of the circle that she ended up having a connection with him by winning this award.

Janet, who has been with the library since 2004, was able

to direct the $10,000 prize money to the library, instead of keeping it for herself. She says that it will go toward the library's This is Red Campaign, which is raising a million dollars for the library, one penny at a time. They have around $18,000 including the prize money.

This was an essential donation considering the lack of live events due to the shut down in 2020. "I think that she felt really good about that," Keith said.

It is very draining to run the library, anyway, even when she started out and was healthy as she's ever been. It was hard back then. Because she has to run the library, now, with this mental handicap, that she has, it drains her physical energy, but it also drains her morale. So, because of this boost in her morale, she is just able to believe in herself more and she will be able to keep going that much longer.

As far as the future goes, Janet says that she just turned sixty-four and her goal is to leave the library in good physical and financial condition before she retires and turns it over to someone else. She also wants to make sure that any issues or problems are solved as well, along with having money in the bank.

Janet says, "I appreciate the community for the support that they have given me and the library for the receipt of the award. I have received very kind comments."

Keith's advice to those who are shooting to reach their goals is "Where you are from doesn't have anything to do with it." The thing that makes the biggest difference is simple persistence. "Just last week, I was listening to the audio book of The Success Principles which is by Jack Canfield, who helped create *Chicken Soup for the Soul.* One of the illustrations in that book says to aim to do five things every day to further your goal. Small town, big town, doesn't matter, almost everybody has to work hard toward something. The secret is to just keep at it. That's what I would advise. Just keep at it."

Keith and Janet Eldred

Keith says that every time that he talks about Janet, he mentions that she is a hero to him. She inspires him. She is super tough. He tends to be a very confident person and he is willing to just keep at it and she is not confident. To him, that makes her all the more heroic because she has weaknesses. Sometimes, she kind of puts things in her own way because of her lack of confidence, but she just keeps on going.

Janet adds, "We have been open about my condition. We are able to laugh about it. We are doing the best that we can. We hope to be an encouragement to other people with similar conditions."

Just recently, PA State Representative Jim Gregory delivered to Janet and the library, The Commonwealth of Pennsylvania House of Representatives Citation for her library work and The Lemony Snicket Award.

**Portions of this article were previously published in an article written by Eric Shields for The Hollidaysburg Herald and Morrison Cove Herald, published in July 2021
**Information for this article was obtained through a phone interview with Janet Eldred and an in-person interview with Keith Eldred
**Photos were taken by author Eric Shields

ED FLANAGAN

ED FLANAGAN

Altoona's Ed Flanagan came from an athletic family. His dad played semi-pro football both in New York and with The Altoona Mountaineers and even tried out with the Pittsburgh Steelers and his uncle was another football great from Altoona, Steve Lach, who made the Steelers roster in 1940. On the last day of training camp, he suffered an ankle injury and was put on the Steelers taxi squad. He was sent to play for the Long Island Indians where he was coached by the great Benny Friedman. He was then drafted into the Army where he spent five years during World War II. Lach was inducted into the College Football Hall of Fame in 1980 and was an All American at Duke and set the Steelers single season touchdown record in 1947. That record stood for thirty years until Franco Harris broke it in 1976. It isn't any wonder that Flanagan took up the sport as well.

It all started for Ed as a child. He played fullback for Our Lady of Lords in fifth, sixth, seventh and eighth grades. Then, he went to Keith Junior High, where he continued to play fullback. Then, it was on to Altoona High School, where he played for legendary Altoona coach Earl Strohm.

Strohm told him, "Ed, you're a good football player, but I don't think you are going to make it as a fullback." He continued wtih, "We are going to have to change your position."

Ed responded, "What do you need coach?"

Strohm said, "Well, you're dad played center and he won the blanket award. So, I think that we will try to make you a center."

During his Sophomore and Junior years, he spent his time learning to play center. He was not a starter until his senior year, when he was going to be the starting center. Coach Strohm and his line coach Ron Rickens came to him and said that they have a kid who is a little bigger than him, but he is not as strong or quick. So, they moved Ed to Offensive Tackle. During his senior year, he became the starting offensive tackle. That year, he made the all-star team consisting of local players.

As far as college goes, he visited the University of Pittsburgh. Mike Ditka was a senior there at the time. He told Flanagan, "Ed, if they offer you a scholarship, come here. It is a good school."

The next school that he visited was Memphis State. They offered him a scholarship. While he was there, a couple of the guys took him out to where Elvis was playing. The king would play football with the players at times. Elvis would also invite the players to his parties, to make sure that nobody would get into a fight or anything.

He later visited Purdue University. Don Fuoss, who was from Altoona, was the line coach there. Flanagan talked to the head coach and asked how the scholarship program worked. The coach said that he would have a four-year scholarship and the only way that you would lose it is if you would quit or fail. He signed with Purdue.

Fuoss, who was a great coach, was fundamentally sound. "He really helped me. I was a tackle when I got to Purdue." Then, he adds when he got there, as a freshman, they said, "All of the tackles over here." Flanagan ran over to the tackle line. At the time he was about 6'2" 185 pounds. He looked at the line of tackles and they were all 6'4"-6'5" and about 230. "I looked and said 'I don't belong in this line' ". Then they yelled, "Guards over here." Flanagan says that he ran over to the guard line. "I figured that if I could play tackle,

I could play guard. I ran over to play guard and I looked at the guards and they were all shorter than I was and heavier than I was. Then, I thought that this doesn't look like my line." Then, they yelled, "Centers over here." So, Ed ran over to the center line. All of the centers were about as tall as he was and they were about fifteen to twenty pounds heavier. "I figured that I could eat my way into this position. So, I went back to being a center during my freshman year of college."

Though he didn't start at Purdue until his senior year, at the end of the year, he was named team captain. He also played in the Senior Bowl and the Blue-Gray game.

Flanagan graduated with a BA in Physical Education and history.

Then came the draft. He was the third choice in the fifth round for the Detroit Lions. He started as a rookie and played for Detroit for ten years. During that time, he made four pro-bowls, was a member of the All-rookie team, was team captain for five years and was team player rep.

It was exciting for Flanagan to find out about his first trip to the pro-bowl. He said that they were out in LA when the owner of their team William Clay Ford was walking with his son, William Clay Ford Jr, who is now on the board of directors for the Lions and The Ford Motor Company, and he saw me, grabbed me and pulled me aside and said, "Ed, I am going to tell you something and I don't want you to tell anybody." He said, "In two weeks, you're going to be named to the pro-bowl."

After his ten years with the Lions, he was traded to San Diego and started two years there, after which he retired as a player. After that, he became a coach, starting with the USFL's Oakland Invaders and was with them in '84 and '85. The second year, the team went to the finals and played The Baltimore Stars. Baltimore won 28-24. The USFL was a summer league. In order to avoid player fatigue, Flanagan came up with the concept of rotating offensive linemen so that every player got a chance to play.

He later owned a couple of businesses in San Diego, including a printing business. He was also president of the Kearny Mesa Rotary and was the president of The Grand Terrace Chamber of Commerce in California. He was also a member of the National Football League's Players Association.

During his coaching career, he coached about a half dozen teams in the Arena Football League. "One thing that I learned about being a coach is that you're only as good as your head coach. If he gets fired, you're fired," Flanagan adds.

Some of the places where he coached included:

1. San Bernardino Sheriff's Department Team as Head Coach and Offensive Line Coach. They were city champs.

2. San Gorgonio High School as Offensive Line Coach

where they were CIF Finalists.

3. San Bernardino Valley College as Offensive Line Special Technique Advisor.

4. Chaffey College as Offensive Line Coach, Football Academic Advisor and Phys Ed Instructor. They were Ford of Upland champions.

5. Arizona Western College as Offensive Line Coach and Career Development Coordinator.

6. The New York City Hawks of the Arena Football League as Offensive Line/Running Back Coach

7. Milwaukee Mustangs of The Arena Football League as Offensive/ Defensive Line Coach.

8. San Diego Riptide of the Arena Football League as Assistant Head Coach and Offensive/Defensive Line Coach.

9. Arizona Rattlers of the Arena Football League where he was the Offensive Line Coach and Running Backs Coordinator. They went to the post-season division playoffs in 2006.

10. New Mexico Highlands University as the Offensive Line Coach. He was Coach of the Year in 2006.

11. Ft Lewis College as Offensive Line Coach.

12. Fairbanks Grizzlies of the Arena Football League as Offensive Line Coach.

13. Cedar Rapids Titans of the Arena Football League as

Offensive Line Coach.

14. Dodge City Law of the Arena Football League as Offensive Line Coach.

Flanagan says that during his long coaching career, his wife Tina was supportive and adventurous during those years. He retired from coaching in 2016.

Flanagan was born in California when his dad was stationed there in the US WWII Army 1940-1945. "Then, we moved back to Altoona and I was raised here." His dad was a Blair County commissioner for about twenty years. "He was a good dad to have, and he taught me football."

His father would take him out to the alley with the football. There was a telephone pole there, where his father would stand. He taught him how to snap the ball for punts and extra points. When his dad wasn't there, he would put two marks on the pole and for extra points, he would go about seven yards and he would snap and try to hit the marks on the telephone pole. That would be where the hands would be. Then, for a punt, he would go back about fourteen yards and snap and try to hit the mark.

Earl Strohm explained to Ed, "Your dad played center and I am sure that he can teach you how to play." Ed recalls, "I liked Strohm. He was a great guy. He was an easy guy to get along with. He didn't yell and scream. He brought in Ron Rickens, who was a great line coach. He helped to teach me to play center. During my senior year, he taught me how to play offensive tackle, too. Rickens was a great coach as well."

Flanagan also wrestled in the regionals at the Jaffa Mosque. He lost to a Vucullo from Lock Haven who won the state finals. When he went to Purdue, he wrestled there as well. He says that a lot of people don't know this, but his coach had it all set up that if he didn't make it in the NFL, he was going to go to New York to become a pro wrestler. Ed recalls that they were going to call him Irish Ed Flanagan. They were going to put him in a green cape with a shamrock on it. Flanagan's response was, "Coach, I think that I am going to try the NFL first." Ed laughed and said, "Thank God, I made it."

"I think it definitely helped me." That is what Flanagan said in regards to growing up in Altoona. He adds that the coaches he had there, including both Strohm and Rickens were great. He says that all of the coaches that they had were really good and they took it seriously. They would not allow a lot of grief to go on. "I was really pleased to come from Altoona."

Some famous football players had come from Altoona, including his uncle Steve Lach. Lach went to Duke and then played for the Steelers. Flanagan says that a lot of good players came out of Altoona because the coaching staff was so great.

Lach would go and visit when Flanagan played for Our Lady of Lords. He taught Ed how to punt. He would also help Ed's teammates as well. Ed recalls, "Uncle Steve was just a great individual." Lach would later own a bar on 24th street in Altoona.

As far as advice for others, Flanagan says, "When I was a coach, I would tell the players and I would tell the kids, now, first, you have got to work hard and practice. You got to study your playbook because you don't want to make any mistakes. You don't want to jump offsides. You don't want any stupid penalties that you're going to make. So, you have to be smart. You have to play smart. You have to help your teammates and you have got to win as a team. Never give up. Help your teammates when they need it." He adds, "You have got to work hard and you have got to think hard, along with no foul language and no fighting."

Flanagan was inducted into the Blair County Sports Hall of Fame in 1987. Both his mom and dad were there to support him.

**Information for this article was obtained through a phone interview with Ed Flanagan
**Photos were provided by Ed Flanagan

JARED FREDERICK

JARED FREDERICK

By the time that Altoona native Jared Frederick graduated from Bishop Guilfoyle in 2006, he had already established in his mind that he wanted to do something with history. He had known since fourth or fifth grade that he wanted to make a career in history.

There were a number of factors that led him down that path. A major one was that he saw the movie Gettysburg when he was seven years old. That made him conscious of the fact that there was such a thing as history.

"I had always been interested in stories about Abraham Lincoln, George Washington and Martin Luther King Jr. Seeing the movie Gettysburg, really opened up my eyes to the scope and power that historical stories convey," he explained.

Throughout his elementary and middle school years, while of his friends were going to Disneyland and Myrtle Beach, his parents took him to historical sites such as civil war battlefields. That further nurtured his appreciation. "Neither one of my parents were history buffs but they wanted to accommodate my interests and lead me to my life's vocation."

When he was in about eighth grade, they went on a family trip to Gettysburg and he was browsing some of the books in one of the gift shops, books for kids more specifically. He turned to his mom and said he could write something better. "I prided myself on being a decent illustrator. So, my mom said, 'Why don't you do something better?'"

He took that challenge. His sophomore year of high school, he self-published his first book. It was an examination of Civil War Generals. There were concise biographies scattered throughout and then he did an illustration of each general as well. It was meant for young adults and was meant to be a coloring book.

One thing led to another, and he wrote and illustrated a sequel, which was published his senior year of high school. Two years later, he did a similarly illustrated book on the history of Pennsylvania.

Starting in high school and continuing through his college years, he sold ten thousand copies of those three books. That was his summer job. He says that some kids work at the car wash or the grocery store, meanwhile he traveled around the mid-Atlantic going to museums, reenactments and commemorative events and he would sell his books.

"I certainly stood out in a crowd when I did book signings with other authors." They were in their forties, fifties and sixties and here he was a sixteen or seventeen year old kid sitting beside them. "I was a bit of a novelty."

Around this same time, he entered the history degree program at Penn State Altoona. "I had and continue to have a real affinity for my home area. I was always interested in local history." A lot of his smaller weekend adventures with his family, they would go to places like the horseshoe Curve, Baker Mansion and Fort Roberdeau. The reenactment at the fort was an annual favorite of his, growing up. All of this only helped fuel his interest.

Penn State Altoona had a fairly new degree program. So, he thought, "Why would I want to go anywhere else?" He started in 2006. He also continued to sell his books and hone his craft and gained a little bit of a following.

In 2009, he applied for a student internship at Gettysburg National Military Park as part of his program requirements. He had done volunteer work with the National Park Service throughout his high school years at Harpers Ferry National Historic Park. He would get into period clothing, put his artistic skills to use, and portrayed an 1860s newspaper correspondent who was going around and drawing what he saw. It was very unique and a lot of fun. He used that volunteerism as a steppingstone toward a broader professional opportunity within the National Park Service.

He wasn't sure about the internship. After all, there were hundreds of people who had applied, and it is one of the most visited historical sites in the country if not the world. "I was one of four lucky students to get one of the spots during the summer of 2009. It was one of the best summers of my life. It was eye opening." It was the first time that he had lived away from home, the first time that he had lived outside of Blair County and it was the first time that he had lived in a house with people other than his own family members. He says that it was just an insightful joy to work there because he met people from all around the world who came to Gettysburg for different reasons. He says that it spoke to the power of the place.

He did a good enough job during his internship that he was asked to come back as a seasonal park ranger during every summer from 2010 to 2013. He developed something like two dozen different walking tours and educational programs. He made friends with a lot of prominent historians in the field, many of whom he is still friends with to this day. "It was some of the best times of my life, where I spent time living and working on America's best known Civil War battlefield."

Frederick says he still keeps his foot in there. He helps them with some programming and brainstorming ideas whenever he is called upon.

Overlapped with his time at Gettysburg, he entered the master's degree program in history at West Virginia University. He did that from fall 2010 to spring 2012. That allowed him to hone his craft further and take a more analytical approach to history and make it applicable and approachable to the masses when they come to historical sites.

"How do you distill complex historical information so that people from all backgrounds can understand it and appreciate it." Frederick believed this is one of the great challenges of working at a historical site.

In 2012, right after he finished his master's degree, he got an adjunct teaching position at Penn State Altoona. So, he was wearing multiple hats simultaneously, for a while. He was park ranger during the summer and a professor during the academic year.

In 2014, he was hired full time at Penn State Altoona. He has been there ever since and has written four more books, focused on local history, civil war history, and various episodes of the second world war.

He says that few people get to have their hobby be their profession. "Very few people in society have that sort of privilege. I'm one of them. I consider myself very lucky in that regard."

Coinciding with his research and his teaching, he is involved with local historical sites over the past several years, particularly Baker Mansion, Fort Roberdeau and more recently The Railroaders Memorial Museum. He often tries to help these organizations by helping them to incorporate some of the latest practices in the history field and he tries to serve as a bridge between those sites and his students and the institution at Penn State Altoona. He tries to nurture a sense of collaboration and partnership that will be mutually beneficial between all those entities and have them work together for a common cause of historical education.

In addition to teaching, Frederick is working on his PhD in American Studies through Penn State Harrisburg.

Frederick adds that his travels have taken him all over the world. He has been to London a few times, has explored the Normandy Battlegrounds in depth and has traveled a good portion of the United States visiting historical sites. He says that he is just getting started and has a lot more to see before his time is up.

In November 2018, Frederick entered a national contest that was to coincide with the 25th anniversary of the tv channel Turner Classic Movies. Basically, you had to submit a video in which you had to pick a movie that is important to you. You also had to dedicate it to someone who is important to you and essentially explain why you are worthy to be a guest host on the Tv channel.

Frederick picked the movie Gettysburg. "I said that this movie made me a historian." He adds that he was able to work at the park as a result of the interest the movie had instilled within him. Frederick was one of the lucky twenty-five winners.

In April 2019, his guest host feature debuted on the tv channel. Frederick sat down and talked about the movie and says that he got to fly to Atlanta and went to Turner studios. He got a behind the scenes look at how a television network is run. "It was a really fascinating once in a lifetime experience."

Frederick is a firm believer that history can and should be taught in spheres beyond the traditional classroom. He adds that historians have an obligation to teach more than just in front of a blackboard. He says that reenacting is a really engaging method of bringing the past to life in a very tangible way. People can see up close and personal when someone has the opportunity to pick up equipment or try on old historical clothing or smell the campfire or the gun powder. This evokes a connection with history that cannot easily be replicated in the classroom.

In 2013, Frederick established The Furious Fourth WWII Living History Association. They recreate the lives of the men of the Fourth Infantry Division who served in World War II.

Frederick's grandfather was a painter for the Pennsylvania Railroad. He served in that outfit during the conflict. "That is why we chose to portray that specific outfit. It's a wonderful means of getting in touch with history in a unique way, while also paying tribute to my grandfather, who passed away when I was five years old. I never had the opportunity to speak to him about his experiences." Frederick and his brother are in the midst of producing a short film about some of his grandfather's exploits during the war. "We are fundraising for that right now. We are hoping to film that motion picture here in the central Pennsylvania area next year."

Frederick wrote and his brother directed the orientation films shown at Fort Roberdeau and Baker Mansion. He adds that his brother is currently an employee at The Railroaders Memorial Museum and he is going to be making some railroading films for them. Frederick is sure that he will be helping with them.

He says that a lot of his contributions to various films and documentaries have been for The National Park Service while he worked there. He has also done a number of on-line presentations and lectures for another organization that he is closely involved with called The American Battlefield Trust. He has been a member of that organization since he was twelve years old.

The mission of the Trust is to buy and preserve American battlefields and to save them from urban sprawl and development and allow them to retain their original historical appearance for the benefit of future generations who might want to visit these sites. Frederick has been a big proponent of their work for a long time and has lent his voice and expertise to some of their projects throughout the years.

Frederick believes that being from Blair County has nurtured his appreciation for history. He adds that there are so many historical sites to be found within an hour drive of Altoona. Frederick says that he had very accommodating and patient parents who were good enough to introduce him to a lot of those places throughout his youth. It really fostered an appreciation for the Blair County area. "By studying Blair County history, I have really become a big advocate of historical preservation."

One of the tragic things about Blair County is how much of its history that we have lost and when you think of all of the grand buildings and structures that we have lost whether it be hotels or railroad buildings or these large structures that once graced downtown Altoona. "So many of them are gone. It is one of the things that really saddens me about Blair County."

As a result, Frederick says that this has inspired and motivated him to raise awareness about the historical treasures that still exist and explain why they are worth saving. "If I have played a small part in allowing people to recognize the treasures in our midst, then I would say that 'it was time well spent.'"

Frederick's advice to others would be, "Don't take the people and history around you for granted. Make the most of the tools, the knowledge and the resources that are at your disposal and use them as a force for good." He says, "Try to retain the history and heritage of your town while also making it a feasible place to live for the future."

The future and the past are joined together at the hip. "I think that when people realize that, then they can use that as a template or a means of inspiration while making their community a happy and livable place to reside."

When talking about some of his goals, Frederick says that ever since he was a teenager, he has kept a notebook of book ideas. He doesn't think that he will be able to write all of them because there are too many. However, he is going to try to write as many as he can. He is going to try to share stories of the past with as many people as possible. "If I can become a best-selling author within the next decade or two as a result, I certainly wouldn't mind that either."

Frederick sums it up by saying, "If you have a passion for something—if you really like history or science or sports—make use of that knowledge and that enthusiasm."

**Information for this article was provided through a phone interview with Jared Frederick
**Photos were provided by Jared Frederick

JIM GREGORY

JIM GREGORY

A Blair County resident since 1985, State Representative Jim Gregory has had a long career in the public eye. Growing up in Latrobe, PA, he wanted to be a sportscaster since he was in the ninth grade. During his high school and college years at Ohio University, he worked to realize that goal and was given the opportunity to achieve it.

In 1985, Gregory was hired by Barb Kooman, the News Director at WTAJ-TV 10. He came to Altoona to work as a part-timer doing weekends with Rodger Wyland.

About a year after that, while working at WTAE in Pittsburgh at the same time, Gregory was offered his first full-time job on air in Champaign, IL. After working at a station there for a year, he received a call from the News Director at WTAJ in July 1986 to come back and replace Rodger Wyland as Sports Director.

Gregory said, "I was amazed that the job was open because I knew that Penn State was going to have a really good football team in '86 and Rodger was a big Penn State fan and an alumnus. However, he wanted to go and so, I came back."

His first year here, he got to cover Penn State's national championship, which he says was "amazing."

Gregory had a lot of amazing opportunities at channel ten for twelve years until the opportunity presented itself to go work with The Altoona Curve, the new AA minor league affiliate of the Pittsburgh Pirates. He accepted that position and was the first employee in 1998. He worked there for a year without a stadium, selling tickets and advertising.

In 1999, they opened the stadium for the inaugural season of Altoona Curve baseball. By 2001, Pennsylvania State Senator Robert Jubelirer was looking for someone to man his staff in the district. The opportunity was too good to pass up. It was a chance to improve life for Gregory's family. "I had never been in politics before. So, I took it. Ironically to this day, that experience in that job pays dividends every day." He adds, "I learned a little bit about what to do and what not do in politics in Senator Jubelirer's office. Those relationships are still helpful to me to this day."

After five years, the senator was voted out of office, and Gregory was looking for a job. he ended up, thanks to some friendships, at Omega Bank for a year and a half as VP of Customer Relation Management. He says that it was an awesome opportunity to learn another industry, which helps him to understand the banking industry to this day with this job. Then, there was a merger between First National Bank and Omega Bank. So, he was left looking for a job again.

He ended up with Jim Forman and ProCare Physical Therapy, doing marketing for them for 7 ½ years. "I learned a lot about healthcare, and I learned a lot about worker's compensation along with a lot about business manufacturing, return to workplace physical therapy and all kinds of good things that actually lend themselves to this job, now."

Jim Gregory on the set of WTAJ TV 10 News

He started his own radio show. He did that for about a year, while he was planning on running for office in 2017. Of course, he ran for his office in 2018, with his first term beginning in 2019. Now, he is currently in his third year in office.

Gregory says being an hour away from his parents, staying in Pennsylvania, bringing his life experiences, contributing to the betterment of his community, the betterment of his family, the betterment of his own personal life and the betterment of Blair County as a community has been truly one of the most fulfilling things that ever happened to him. He adds that it didn't happen, though, for him until he was here for a while.

"I feel like I was taking from Blair County for a lot of the time I had been here and now I feel like I am giving back to Blair County. What I realize as we get older, we only become wiser if we are willing to recognize what is truly important." He has been able to realize over the past fifteen years what really is important about life on this earth is that "We are spiritual beings having a human experience." He adds "My human experience right now is the best that I can possibly ask for. Being able to have that now, in this position, is what makes being in Blair County and the 80th district for me by far is that I can't imagine that there is a better district of people in the Commonwealth than right here in so many ways."

He says the entire time that he has been here, "It has been able to lead me and guide me to recognize what is truly important and be able to lead by some examples, to recognize that we live in a great place, that we should be grateful for what we have here and that, yes, we have our warts but find me a better place in Pennsylvania to live than right here."

He would put this area up against any place in the Commonwealth. There is no place that he would rather be than here. Gregory says the time that he spent experiencing what it is like to work with constituents in Senator Jubelirer's office really gave him a good foundation to recognize what the challenges as the actual elected official were going to be like.

His challenges have been a little different than challenges that someone else may face, who would not have had that opportunity to learn and to know what you are getting yourself into.

He beleives the challenges have really just been to make sure that he is doing the very best that he can to speak for the people of his district, because he is one of 203 and he has been blessed with a voice that people recognize, and he has been blessed with a background that people recognize with his experience on television. He tries to use those experiences to the benefit of the voters and residents of his district to speak for what he thinks that they believe is best for them and for their lives here in Blair County.

Because he has lived there for over thirty-five years and he has been involved in a lot of community endeavors, Gregory says, that he would like to think that he has been able to understand and have a good grasp of what is important to the people here. He adds that if he can take advantage of his storytelling experience and vocalize what the stories of the people of the 80th are all about, then he thinks he is meeting the challenge of speaking for them about what is important as a state representative, speaking for the people of the 80th district.

Gregory mentions that he has been given the chance to go elsewhere but decided to stay here in Central Pennsylvania. He says that he didn't know this back then, but he has learned since then, that nothing happens in God's World by mistake.

"It is no mistake that when I was offered a job to go to Columbus, OH to become the number three sports reporter for the CBS affiliate in that area that I turned it down."

When he looks back on it at times, he has thought about what would have happened.

With all of the things that has happened to him since, he says that he is so grateful that he did not take that job. He contemplates, "What would have happened if I had taken it?" He says that maybe some great things would have happened. "God's plan for me is that I am here. I am just going to keep following where he leads me and so far, he leads me to where I am sitting here with you talking about being a state representative. I am enjoying the heck out of it. I am just grateful that his plan for me has been what it has been and to experience all of the things that I had a chance to experience. It has been truly unbelievable."

As far as the future goes, Gregory says that he is a one day at a time guy. He has a lot of sayings that he tries to live by: "Yesterday is history and tomorrow is a mystery but today is the present and that is why they call it a gift" and "Future plans are what God laughs at us for" are two of them.

He says that because of all of the things that he has experienced since he has lived here, all of those that he has experienced in his life, all of those things that happened for a reason and they have been awesome. So, he can only expect and pray that what happens tomorrow, next week, next month, next year is just going to be a continuation of those things if he continued to believe and be grateful.

"If that is the case, the only thing that I would say to

'What does the future hold for Jim Gregory' is I hope the future continues to hold blessings that I have been given to this point."

When asked about what advice that he would give people growing up in small town Pennsylvania, he says "I think about that answer in terms of what I would tell my own boys. They are both in their mid-twenties. What I tell them and what I want for them is that I just want them to be happy."

Jim Gregory and his wife Lynn Thompson Gregory

His advice would be "be happy with where you are and what you are but don't stop and don't sell yourself short on taking chances, being willing to make mistakes. You learn so much more from failure." He remembers Joe Paterno when he said, "You learn more from a defeat than you do from a victory." He believes that that's the same thing in life.

Gregory said, "Please, please, please don't let failure define you. Let failure guide you to be able to find happiness in the process of reaching your goals." He added, "Because once you reach your goals, that is not your destination. It is the process. The work that you put in, that if you can enjoy what you're doing when you do it. Recognize that everything is a blessing. Be grateful. Take time to recognize the small things and say, 'Thank You' to people along the way.

"Don't ever think that somebody, who is in your life today won't come back into your life a year, ten years or fifteen years from now, because those people are in your life forever. Once God puts them in your path, you're in their path and they are in yours, forever. Just recognize that. That is just such a powerful opportunity to have happiness in your life.

"I wish that I would have learned this when I was younger. 'Don't be afraid to ask for help. No matter what it is. Don't ever feel like you are terminally unique without recognizing what you may be struggling with and troubled with. It is happening to others. Don't think that you are unique and are going to be this way for the rest of your life. The opportunity to ask for help and recognize that you are not alone in your struggles will open doors and opportunities that you can't imagine."

He continued on with, "Another thing that I have learned that is good advice that I wish I learned earlier in my life is 'Don't have a fear of economic insecurity.' That fear if you allow it, will run your life because you will say and do things because it is all about the money and that will bring economic security. If you lose the fear of economic security, it will open up so much more of an opportunity to have economic security. Don't let that run your life. If you don't let that run your life, it is amazing how it comes for you in bountiful blessings."

**Information for this article was obtained through an in-person interview with Jim Gregory
**Photos were provided by Jim Gregory

CAITLIN HARSHBERGER

CAITLIN HARSHBERGER

All-star cheerleader Caitlin Harshberger's routine photo shoot with photographer Mallory Neil ended with a nomination to be in the nationally produced *Inspiring Teens Magazine*. She was nominated by Neil and then voted on by the public.

The money was raised through the voting process was deposited into a fund, which was put into a scholarship for the two winners, which included *The Inspiring Teen Style* winner, which she won this year. The Scholarship will go toward her college education.

According to their website, Inspiring Teens is a "by teens for teens" organization overseen by adults. They focus on leadership and volunteering. The Inspire Team is a group of teens from around the world. The magazine is run by The Inspire Team.

In addition to attending Altoona Area High School, Caitlin is an All-star Cheerleader at Xtreme Allstars and coaches three teams (Tiny Novice Tanks, Tiny Level 1 Troopers, and Mini Level 1 Majors) that are younger than her. She also competes on two teams, the Senior Level 3 Lady Legends and Senior Level 5-Lady X.

The thing that she loves the most about cheer is the passion that grows in you throughout the years. She says cheer has taught her many life lessons and has shown her how to cope with things in real life. The friendships that she has made along the way are the people who she knows will stick by her on her best and worst days. She also loves seeing the younger athletes grow into the athlete she is today.

Her passion for cheer has impacted her life by teaching her to never give up on herself because hard work always pays off in the end. "Anytime that I have spare time, it is most likely used for mat time, and I would not trade it for the world."

Her dream has always been to be on the best team possible. She is on a level five team for the 2020-21 season. She has won twelve national titles in the 2019-2020 season as well as both at large bids and paid bids to the D2 summit, grand national championships, specialty awards, leaderboard ranking for the D2 Summit, and was personally awarded athlete of the month and best role model. One of her favorite moments so far was walking on to the D2 Summit floor for the first time in 2017.

The D2 Summit is a world championship where teams from all around the world compete. Harshberger says that you must receive a bid, either paid or an at-large bid, to go to the competition. The past two years she has received a paid bid, which means they pay a full ride for you to go. The past two years, all eligible teams from her gym have got a bid to compete. Unfortunately, due to COVID, they did not hold the D2 Summit Competition this past May in Orlando, Florida.

To be included in the magazine means that people think that Harshberger is a good role model for people in her gym and that her hard work has paid off.

Harshberger is very involved in academics at school including National Honor Society and Student Council. She likes to not only achieve her goals but to do the best she can with them. Managing schoolwork and cheer have been challenging for her throughout the years, but schoolwork always comes first. She adds that long nights after cheer consist of doing homework on her one hour drive to the gym, staying up past midnight to finish projects, studying with her friends in the car, and also taking extra work with her to competitions to finish for the days that she had missed.

Harshberger is very dedicated, responsible and motivated to reach her goals in life. She has put a lot into cheer and school and because of that she is able to fulfill her dreams. She thinks that it is important to have structure in your life in order to meet your goals and achieve great things.

The hardest thing that she has ever accomplished was telling herself to never give up after hard times. Her Nannie passed away in 2018 and they were inseparable. After her passing, Harshberger thinks she could let herself move on in cheerleading and in school. When she goes through rough times where she doubts herself, but she remembers that her Nannie would tell her to keep going. She manages to get through these times by talking with her friends and being at the cheer gym really helps. The cheer gym has always been a place where she can release stress and feel better. She also looks back on pictures of her Nannie and that helps show her how proud she was of her.

Caitlin's mom, Mindy Despot, adds that during the past two years, Caitlin has been through a lot of heartache. When she lost her Nannie, who was her best friend and biggest role model, Caitlin was crushed. She also lost her Great Grandmother and Great Grandfather this past year and with COVID interrupting everyone's life, she wasn't able to be at the gym and school. Despot says, "I can say this kid always has a smile on her face, always there to help, always doing the best that she can in everything that she does and is always trying to lift everyone up around her. She is a true

Caitlin and her nannie

inspiration to me, and I couldn't be prouder of the young lady she is becoming."

Harshberger has been dating her boyfriend for four years

now and she says that he always supports her and is there for her when she is having a bad day.

Mom's advice to other parents is to be their number one supporter. "When they make mistakes or they fail, always be there to pick them up." She adds that criticism goes both ways-good and bad. She says that you need to attend every event that you can and anything that is going on in their lives, be front and center. That way, they know that you are 100% there.

Caitlin Harshberger 's advice to others is to believe in yourself and don't worry about what others say. Her favorite quote is, "There will be obstacles. There will be doubters. There will be mistakes. However, with hard work, there are no limits." She adds that if you feel that you have reached your limit, keep trying because you can always do better.

Mom says, "I am very proud of the young woman that she has become. The last fifteen years in all-star cheer is a passion of hers. I have watched her grow from the little girl who watched all of those bigger girls saying, 'I want to be just like them' to the girl who all the little girls are now looking at. I am so excited to watch her achieve all of her goals from school to cheer to normal everyday life. I am also watching her become an excellent role model for these younger girls, who look up to her and couldn't be more blessed."

When asked who inspires her, Caitlin says that she finds

her mom inspiring in many ways. She says that her parents got divorced when she was three and she adds that her mom never misses a moment in her life. "She is always there to help and support me when I need it, the most. I have never doubted my mom is my biggest supporter. She is always helping me and is always there for me no matter what. She is always helping others. She is kind, loving, caring, and is always dedicated and focused on making everyone feel good." Caitlin adds that she strives to be like her mom because she is dedicated and focused on what she wants and what she needs the most in her life. Nothing can stop her from reaching her goals.

©Mallory Neil

As far as the future goes, Harshberger says she is planning on going to college and study to become a Physician's Assistant, specializing in Pulmonology. She remembers that this has been a dream of hers for many years. She is hoping to attend Saint Francis University. After that, she plans on getting married, having children, and living a happy life.

Caitlin says that she has always been told that she is an inspiration to many of the younger athletes who are around her. This means a lot to her because she loves being a part of their growth in the cheerleading world. She feels that she is inspiring because she rises above her limits. She says that she tries to be a role model for others and show them how much their value is worth. Caitlin says that she strives for perfection in everything that she does. If she struggles with something in life, she works 100% harder to reach that goal. She says, "Always believe in yourself and you will be unstoppable!!"

Caitlin says that she would not be where she is today without her mom, family, and her coaches (Coach Steph, Coach Alex, Coach Pat and Coach Karin). They all push her to be the best she can be.

**Information for this article was obtained through phone interviews with Caitlin Harshberger and Mindy Despot.
**The Cheer photos were provided by and copywritten by Mallory Neil
**Photo of Caitlin and her nannie was provided by Caitlin Harshberger

FRED IMLER SR.

FRED IMLER SR. AND THE IMLER FAMILY

"He was a Shriner's Shriner." Dan Kindle, Jaffa recorder said of Fred Imler Sr.

"Anything that supported the kids, he was always there." Kristin Bigelow, former 4H educator said.

"Fred always had a smile on his face," Joe Hurd, President/CEO of The Blair County Chamber of Commerce, said.

"His family was very important to him. He considered everybody that he worked with everyday to be part of his extended family," his grandson Bryan Imler said.

Fred Imler Sr , who passed away January 12, 2021, was very giving and had received many awards for his work and philanthropy, according to Bryan Imler.

One of those awards includes The Chamber's Lifetime Achievement award. He and Imler's Poultry had just recently been awarded the Agriculture Community Excellence Award, as well.

Imler's Poultry is a long time member of The Chamber. According to Hurd, Fred has certainly been an integral part of so many of the things that The Chamber has sponsored. "He was just an ideal Chamber member in terms of understanding the importance of having the business community help to accomplish things within the local economy."

Fred was a board member of The Shriners Hospital in Philadelphia for a number of years. He would attend the board meetings on a monthly basis. According to Bryan, there were a number of local children that he facilitated their care.

Kindle adds that Fred, who joined the Shriners on May 24, 1969, used to drive to Philadelphia in his own vehicle and deliver eight or nine hundred pounds of chicken and take it to the hospital. "That was the kind of guy he was," Kindle said.

He was also an avid supporter of the Blair County 4H program, the 4H members as well as the area FFA chapters and members.

Kristin Bigelow, who was the 4H educator for the county for about five or six years, says that Fred was always supportive in a variety of ways. Imler's Poultry made some gifts to the 4H endowment. Fred also sponsored awards and he was super supportive in supporting the kids through the livestock auction.

According to Peggy Mock, Blair County Junior Livestock Treasurer, Fred also bought animals and donated to the scholarship fund that they give to members when they are done with school and are headed to college.

Bryan says that Fred was on the board of The Central Pennsylvania Community Foundation for twenty-one years and was treasurer for fourteen of those years. He was also a member of The Hollidaysburg Lions Club and The Grace United Church of Christ in Altoona where he attended since he was a young child.

Bryan says that Fred really enjoyed horses. He was a founding member of The Fort Fetter Riding Club in Duncansville.

Kindle adds that Fred was a member of The Jaffa Mounted Patrol unit. "He rode in all of the parades," he adds.

Bryan said that Fred was actively involved in all facets of the business. Up until a couple of weeks before his passing, he still worked everyday including Saturdays and Sundays.

When Fred was younger, he worked at Imler's booth at the Farmers Market in downtown Altoona. After that market had closed, he worked at the farmer's market where the Hoss's is located at in Altoona. "He had a passion for the retail side of the business," Bryan says of his grandfather. He adds that Fred was also involved in writing the weekly newspaper ad. Fred would also go to The Morrison Cove produce auction to support them and the local growers and then would offer their items through Imler's retail stores as well as to their wholesalers.

Imler's Poultry had its beginnings back close to the turn of the last century. In 1903, Leff Imler (Fred Sr's Great Great Uncle) operated a General Store in Rainsburg, Bedford County.

About 1915, Charles Imler (Fred Sr's Grandfather) purchased the business and continued with the operation. In 1918, Charles and Minty Imler moved the business and the family to 58th street in Altoona. He continued to do business with the farmers in Friends Cove, Bedford County.

When Charles passed away in 1940, his son Lester assisted his mother in operations of the business. By this time, they were bringing poultry from West Virginia to be processed and sold by both wholesale and retail. During this time, Minty retired and Lester became the owner.

In 1947, they began a turkey growing operation locally on sixth avenue road. This is the time that Fred Imler Sr had been working at the Farmers Market.

In 1951, after Fred's graduation, he became a partner in the business with his brother Richard and father Lester. In addition to several retail locations, the wholesale business covered about a fifty mile radius of Altoona.

Lester Imler died in 1968 and Richard and Fred Sr. operated as partners until 1977. At that time, Richard wanted to devote all of his time to his Agway business and Fred Sr purchased his interest and real estate.

Fred Imler II, the son of Fred Sr, was involved working in the business and after Fred Sr had resolved the buyout, Fred II became a partner in the business.

After the 1979 growing season, Fred II convinced Fred Sr to discontinue the growing and slaughtering of turkeys.

Fred II wanted to move the focus of the business to expanding the business distribution volume.

During this time Karen Imler, daughter of Fred Sr, was working at the Farmers Market. As the business continued to grow, she became active in the daily office operations.

In 1980, the business name changed from Imler's Turkey Farm to Imler's Poultry.

In 1983, they were awarded distribution of approximately fifty Kentucky Fried Chicken locations, which dramatically increased their distribution area.

With an increase in sales staff in 1984, a red meat and full deli line were added to the product list. The business moved to 3421 Beale Avenue in Altoona.

In 1992, Imler's Poultry Transportation Inc was formed. Now, Imler's not only hauled their products but they also started in the outside hauling business.

In June of 1999, Imler's was awarded the USDA bid for distribution of government commodities to the Southwest Region of Pennsylvania and June of 2000, the Northwest Region of Pennsylvania was secured.

In July 2010, the business moved to its current facility on Rte 764.

Now with Fred's passing, there will be some big shoes to fill.

"There were a lot of kids that were pretty close to Fred and enjoyed the opportunity to sit down and talk with him. He was kind of one of those guys who had a wealth of knowledge to share. Anytime you finished a conversation with him, you felt a little bit wiser," Bigelow said.

Bryan adds "For me personally, he instilled a tremendous work ethic in me. He had an honorable way of doing business. He was forthright in delivering our promises to our customers. He was a great leader and mentor to everybody here,"

**Portions of this article were previously written by Eric Shields for The Morrison Cove Herald newspaper in January 2021
**Information for this article was obtained through phone interviews with Dan Kindle, Kristin Bigelow, Joe Hurd, Bryan Imler and Peggy Mock. Some information for this article was also obtained from the Imler's Poultry website.
**Photo was provided by Bryan Imler

JOLENE KOPRIVA

JOLENE KOPRIVA

Upon graduating Duquesne University in the 1970s, the Honorable Judge Jolene Kopriva had no intentions on returning to her hometown of Hollidaysburg, Pennsylvania for work.

As fate and God's will would have it, that all changed. Kopriva graduated from Penn State in 1975 with a major in law enforcement and corrections. She wasn't sure if she was going to get into law school, but she did, and it was off to Pittsburgh and Duquesne. It was during those three years that she made the decision that she would probably want to stay in Pittsburgh. However, when she graduated, she couldn't find a job in the city. There were not many women being hired there.

Kopriva grew up in Hollidaysburg, where she had babysat for Clyde Black, who was a partner in a local law firm. She says that she had approached him, when she was contemplating law school, and asked if women were attorneys. He told her that there were three of them in Blair County. It was that interaction with Attorney Black that helped her to start thinking about law school.

Then, in his law firm, Marion Patterson, the founding attorney had passed away suddenly. It was then that his firm was looking to hire a new attorney. That is when Black approached her parents and asked if Kopriva had secured a job, yet. They told him, "No."

After an interview, they hired her. She begrudgingly returned to Hollidaysburg because she didn't have another job and she needed a paycheck. "I was the first female at the firm," she said. "Little did I know that they would give me tremendous opportunities." Her career has been really mapped out for her. "I always thought that God had a plan for me. I didn't know it at the time."

Kopriva says that her plan was to work there and then go back to Pittsburgh when a job became available.

She explained that the law school class at Duquesne had a quota the year she started in 1975. They wanted one third women. There were more women in her class than had ever graduated from the law school since it had started. She says that they were really making a commitment to equalize the playing field.

Once joining the law firm, most of her challenges came from the older attorneys. She said that people called her "girly". One attorney said to her, "What are you doing here? If I wanted to see a woman, I would go home and see my wife."

She admits that it was hard, but the firm gave her every opportunity they gave the males. One partner who, when she would return from a court hearing in Bedford or Huntingdon, asked, "Did they like you?" He didn't ask if she won or lost, only if they liked her.

Though, there were different nuances that were interesting, they made her stronger and more appreciative. One of her colleagues told her one time, "You're lucky. I am just one of many men. If I want to distinguish myself, I would have to do something spectacular. All you have to do is show up because you're a woman." That helped Kopriva get a perspective.

In order to distinguish herself as a woman, she had to work a little harder which she says is okay. She had to prove herself that she was capable. Kopriva adds, "I like people and a lot about being a lawyer is getting the trust of people and understanding people and I think I worked hard at that and enjoyed that part of my job. I always tried to do my best

and I think that if you're listening to people, they will trust you."

"I was able to help people. That is why I wanted to be an attorney. I wanted to help people." Word got around that she helped this person and then other people came. "I had a successful run as an attorney."

Kopriva's transition from attorney to judge began as a result of a time of eight years where Blair County went through an incredible turnover of judges. There was an early retirement, a judge who died of cancer, a judge who was charged with molestation of his stepchildren, along with a sudden death. There were a lot of things going on.

Kopriva adds that there was another female attorney who kept running for judge. Different people kept telling her, "If there should be a woman judge, it should be you." And the seed was planted.

The opportunity came about with the sudden death of Bert Leopold. He had run in the primary against a female attorney. He won and he was the walk through candidate for November. In July, he was swimming at the gym, crawled out of the pool and died of a sudden heart attack. The Republican party named a candidate, and the Democrats also named a candidate. The Republican party was split, it was a bitter race in the spring between Bert Leopold and his opponent. His opponent thought that since he had died, it should be hers. As a result, there was four way race and the committee people voted. Kopriva was the dark horse candidate and ended up winning.

Judge Kopriva related her feelings about being the first female judge in Blair County, "I had been an attorney for ten years. At that point, I had to come to think of myself as Jolene, not a male or female. I just loved the work of law and I loved helping people. I thought being a judge would give me a different framework to do that." She worked hard to campaign and let people know who she was as an individual and tried not to think about the male-female thing.

However, once she took office, it still followed her. A local newspaper reporter would come to the courtroom to watch her to see if she was going to cry. The newspaper articles would be contradictory. If Kopriva gave someone probation, they would say, "Judge Kopriva was soft on defendant." If a male judge would do the same, the papers would say that the judge gives guy a chance.

"You survive, you get stronger with it. You learn about yourself. For me, it became a journey of faith. When you're a judge, it is a lonely position. You ultimately have to make the decision your own and live with it. I always say God and I got very close."

When talking about highlights of her career, she says that there are so many good memories. "I love my work. I love my career. I can't imagine anything that would have suited me better." One thing that is still a part of her life is drug court. "To help folks, who are during addiction and treat them with the opportunity to transform their lives and treating it as more of a disease with accountability. That was very rewarding work."

Judge Kopriva's advice for those who have big goals is to do what you love to do. Follow that and learn what you're good at and what you enjoy. Then, success just comes. She adds, "Be the best person you can be. *That* is success." You might be someone who works in a school doing maintenance or working in the cafeteria. However, if you are the best cafeteria worker or the best maintenance person, then you are doing what God has intended because you are using your gifts. "You never know where that is going to take you."

"I didn't start out wanting to be a judge." She just decided that this was the path that she wanted. She wanted to help people. She wanted to be in law. Everything just sort of flowed.

Jolene Kopriva and her husband Tom

Currently, Kopriva says that she and her husband Tom are enjoying retirement. She adds that she is a senior judge. She works about three or four days a month. She says that she still enjoys helping others. She didn't leave because she was tired of the job, but rather because she was sixty-four and terms are ten-year terms and she didn't want to work until she was seventy-four. She still enjoys going into work. Kopriva adds that they have also committed to helping with their grandchildren.

Looking back on her career, she remembers that there were many times that she had to accept the responsibilities of her job and ended up missing her children's events. When her daughter walked around the swimming pool on senior night at the high school, she was in Florida training for drug court.

She is finding lots of things to do including reading and helping neighbors and friends. She is also is very active in their church. She gets up every day and asks, "Where do you want me today, God? We are blessed in many ways."

**Information for this article was obtained through an in-person interview with Jolene Kopriva
**Photos were provided by Jolene Kopriva

PAT MALONE

PAT MALONE

Local baseball historian, Tom Sipes, believes that Altoona native and former major leaguer Pat Malone was destined to be enshrined in the Baseball Hall of Fame in Cooperstown. However, Sipes said Malone liked to drink too much and that probably affected his chances.

As a kid, Malone didn't like his given name of Perce. He said that it sounded too "sissy" and demanded that it be changed to Pat. He was a leader of a gang of boys who stole food from neighbors and took it to a nearby shanty where they concocted their next plan.

By the age of fourteen, he had quit school and was working for the parcel carrier Adams Express. He later falsified his age to land a job as a fireman on the Pennsylvania Railroad at the age of sixteen. A year later, he enlisted in the Us Army. He played football and baseball in the army. He also boxed while in the service.

Upon returning to Altoona, he fought forty-one professional fights, mostly at the Jaffa Mosque, under the name of Kid Williams. He also had a short stint as a football player at Juniata College in Huntingdon. He, then had success as a pitcher for the semipro Altoona Independents.

After compiling a 13-12 record in 219 innings with the Knoxville Pioneers, John McGraw and the New York Giants bought Malone for a reported $5,000. After a suspension from the Giants, he was later given a second chance with them. He ended up being discarded by McGraw because of his wayward behavior. They sold Malone to the Minneapolis Millers of the American Association.

At twenty-one years of age, Malone had already established his reputation as a swashbuckler who was busy wasting his talents. His record for his first five seasons of professional baseball was 44-66.

During his season with The Des Moines Demons of the class A Western League in 1926, he had a league leading 190 strikeouts, a career high in wins with twenty-eight and innings with 349 while becoming one of the most unhittable pitchers in the league. Malone helped to lead the Demons to the league title.

When pitching for the Millers in 1927, he continued to prove himself by leading the American Association in strikeouts with 214. He ranked in the top five in almost every important pitching category including twenty wins, 319 innings and fifty-three games.

Malone was then sold to the Cubs for a reported $25,000. He proved to be the Cubs most successful and consistent pitcher especially during the pennant race in the last two months of the 1928 season. He won nine of ten decisions in August and September, hurling complete games in eight of his last nine starts. He relieved four other games and notched a 2.41 ERA in 89 2/3 innings. His 155 strikeouts and 5.56 strikeouts per nine innings were second only to Brooklyn Robins ace, Dazzy Vance.

In 1929, the Cubs won their first pennant since 1918 behind the league's best pitching trio of Malone, Charlie Root and Guy Bush, who won a combined 59 games. An associated press story suggested that Malone had "probably the fastest ball in the major leagues". He held the strikeout title with a career best of 166.

In 1930, Malone led the league with twenty wins and twenty-two complete games. He also had personal bests with 45 appearances, 35 starts and 271 2/3 innings.

The relationship between Malone and Rogers Hornsby, the new Cubs manager, started off poorly in 1931 and only worsened throughout the season.

The season did not go well. From 1928 to 1932, he averaged eighteen wins and 251 innings. Malone helped lead the Cubs to the NL pennant in both 1929 and 1932.

Malone was described as an "overgrown boy" and prankster who played practical jokes on everybody around him. Sportswriter Frank Graham called him, "One of the most popular players ever to wear a Cubs uniform…who never let his fans down."

He was a vocal clubhouse leader and supportive teammate. He was also temperamental, upset easily by umpires or fans razzing him. He needed a gentle coaxing from a supportive manager.

General manager William Veeck paid the expenses for Malone's wife to accompany the team on road trips to chaperone him. By 1931, roommates Hack Wilson and Malone were inseparable drinking buddies with reputations as barroom brawlers.

The low point of Malone's career came on September fifth when he beat up two sportswriters in a pullman wagon in Cincinnati while Wilson looked on. Hornsby was livid and vowed that "Wilson and Malone will not be with my ballclub in 1932." Malone was fined $500.

According to *Fouled Away*, a biography of Hack Wilson, he and Malone began drinking heavily after Wilson had been benched for poor play after that game in Cincinnati.

"The next day, they woke up like angry bears. Waiting at the train station to return to Chicago, both players encountered Harold Johnson of the Chicago American and Wayne K. Otto of the Herald Examiner.

"One account claims that Johnson taunted Malone by saying, "I've just had a chat with Moredecai Brown. Did you ever hear of him, Pat? He was a great pitcher in his time." Other accounts say that Wilson got into a quarrel with the writers before Malone happened along.

"In any event, it seems well-established that Malone decked Johnson with a right fist to the head. At this point, Otto yelled, "You can't get away with that Malone" and jumped in. Malone also pummeled him. Eyewitnesses including Cubs rushed to pull them apart. Hack did nothing to pull Malone off of the writers and was suspected of encouraging the pitcher in the beating. Later, Malone said the writers deserved the thrashing because they'd been 'on me' in their columns."

Malone pitched complete victories in his next three starts. He finished with sixteen victories. In 1932, Malone won fifteen games and for the fifth consecutive and final time in his career logged at least two hundred innings with

237. He also lost a career high seventeen games.

After his start on August 24th, Malone was mysteriously pulled from the starting rotation and made just two relief appearances the rest of the season. The Cubs kept quiet on the subject, but Malone publicly berated the team, claiming that his unofficial suspension was a ploy to rob him of bonuses that he would earn with each win beginning with his fifteenth. "Anywhere will do just as long as it isn't with the Cubs," said Malone when asked where he anticipated playing in 1935.

On Oct 26, 1934, the Cubs sent Malone and cash to the Cardinals for minor league catcher Ken O'Dea. Malone refused to report to the Cardinals after hearing that General Manager Branch Rickey expected him to take a reported 50% salary cut to $5,000. On December 17, 1934, he placed Malone on waivers, and no one claimed him. Malone and Rickey eventually reconciled their differences enabling the pitcher to report to spring training but he was unexpectedly sold on March 26, 1935 to the New York Yankees.

Malone was moved to the Bullpen by the Yankees. He collected eighteen saves during three seasons including an American League lead with nine saves in 1936. Malone won his only championship in the 1936 world series. The Yankees released him in January 1938.

The Minnesota Millers bought Malone's contract. He lasted for only one relief appearance before he abruptly quit the team in April. He had been suspended after a drunken melee at the team's hotel in Indianapolis before opening day.

After Baltimore of the Double A International League purchased his contract, he split the season with the Orioles and the Chattanooga Lookouts of the class A Southern Association. Baltimore sold his contract to the Oakland Oaks of the Double A Pacific Coast League in the off season, but Malone chose to retire on February 20, 1939.

In his ten-year Major League career, Malone won 134 and lost ninety-two. He logged 1,915 innings, recorded 1,024 strikeouts, and posted a 3.74 ERA in 357 appearances including 220 starts, 115 complete games, fifteen shutouts, twenty-six saves, and was on four pennant winners.

As a hitter, Malone recorded a .188 batting average (129 for 688) with nine home runs and sixty-one RBIs. According to the Elias Sports Bureau, he is one of two pitchers in the modern era to hit at least one home run in his first five major league seasons. (1928-32). The other is Dontrell Willis (2003-07).

In 1929, he hit four home runs in 105 at bats. Only two other Cubs pitchers, Fergie Jenkins in 1971 and Carlos Zambrano in 2006, have hit four or more homeruns in a single season.

According to an article written for The Blair County Sports Hall of Fame, Tom Irwin Sr was a young major leaguer with the Cleveland Indians when Malone's career was coming to an end. Once, when the Indians visited Yankee stadium, Irwin met up with his fellow Altoona native.

Irwin says that he didn't know Pat at the time, but he knew that he was from Altoona. "When I took the infield with the Cleveland club, he stood on the sidelines and was giving me encouragement."

After retirement, Malone returned to Altoona with his wife and daughter and opened a bar in downtown Altoona. He died on May 13, 1943 of acute pancreatitis, a disease that can be caused by alcohol abuse. He was forty years old.

**Information for this article was obtained from the following sources:
1. www.sabr.org
2. Wikipedia article on Pat Malone
3. Article written by Neil Rudel for The Blair County Sports Hall Of Fame
4. In-person interview with baseball historian Tom Sipes

RAY J. MCDONALD

RAY J. MCDONALD

"He was a person with goals in mind when he was a child to change things," says Joe McDonald of his father, Ray. Born in Sproul in 1922, Ray J. McDonald had some hills to climb with one being the death of his father at the age of sixteen. Ray had to assist in helping a family of six. That was back in 1938.

McDonald enlisted to go to World War II, he joined the Marines. It was in his third year in battle when he was in The Pacific division and the Japanese blew up the ship. He was blown off the ship. He was missing in action for four days and presumed dead.

Joe says that he was, then, sent to Walter Reed Hospital. This is where his second life changing experience happened. Back in the forties, there was no physical therapy clinics or rehabs for soldiers. It was done by doctors and nurses. Joe says his dad looked at that and said, "This is where I need to be."

McDonald always believed in helping people. With the GI Bill and with the assistance of some people, he spent eight years earning degrees from Penn State University, the Medical College of Virginia and New York University. He was one of the first graduates with a master's degree in Physical Therapy in the United States. Joe says that his father was the first licensed Physical Therapist in Blair County. It was at that point when he was working at the VA Hospital that he saw a child who had Cerebral Palsy. That was his next life changing experience, he turned his life into helping these kids.

McDonald focused the remaining part of his life trying to get these children to walk. There was a non-profit organization called Easter Seals across the United States. He helped to found that organization in the state of Pennsylvania. He opened four clinics in four different counties, including Blair, Bedford, Clearfield, and Lycoming Counties.

Ray McDonald became so well known, they were coming from Pittsburgh and Harrisburg to see him. Dr. Kantz, an orthopedic surgeon out of Philadelphia, specialized in Cerebral Palsy patients. Dr. Kantz would come once a month to see Ray and they would conduct a clinic. People from Pittsburgh to Harrisburg, with children, who have these issues, would make appointments to see his father.

Joe adds that it was rewarding to his father, personally because he was one of those people, who wanted to see the braces come off and have those kids walk. "He was one of those people who looked at things and wanted to see how he can change people's lives for the better."

Joe added, "My mother was a Registered Nurse. She assisted him in the Easter Seals Campaign. She is the one who created this idea and tried to get him into the Claysburg Hall of Fame. She would have been really proud of this, because they were both from Claysburg. They really cherished this town. They thought that the world turned around Claysburg, because it was such a family-oriented town. If she were alive today, she would be so happy."

Joe says that his father was really a small-town guy. "He was never into the high end look at me type of thing. He was one of those people who stayed low key and became well-known for that. He wasn't the type of guy who sought fame and fortune. He was the guy who liked to help people who needed help."

For his time served in the war, Ray received the Purple Heart. "When he enlisted in the Marines, they put him in the clean-up operation when they battled in the islands in the South Pacific. They would go from island to island, and they brought his platoon in and they would do clean up and take out small little pockets of enemy warfare. He was more or less a tunnel rat. He would go into tunnels and things like that and get the enemy," Joe says.

Joe adds that it wasn't anything that he was either proud of or wanted to remember. "Like all WWII Veterans, he very seldom talked about that." He says that it was a tough time because of the injury that occurred during that time because they would bring the boats in on one of the islands. He adds that is when they took the boat out. He was lost at sea for four days.

Toward the end of his career, in the late sixties or early seventies, he also became a sports trainer. There was no such thing at the time. There was only an x-ray that would analyze an injury to a patient. There was no MRIs. Joe says there was a dire need for people to look at things on the field and his dad volunteered his time to local high schools. He would see student athletes. Joe says he saw people such as Wade Schalles, a famous local wrestler. He adds that Mike Reid would come to the house all of the time. In 1976, Ray was the trainer for the big thirty-three classic when it was held locally. Joe says that Dan Marino had a slight injury, so, he came up to the house. "That was the norm to see people like that."

Joe explains, "He was a good man. He was one of those people, who never cared too much about the dollar. He just cared about people. He wanted everybody to have a fair chance in life."

**Information for this article was obtained through a phone interview with Joe McDonald
**Photos were provided by Joe McDonald

CHUCK MONTS

CHUCK MONTS

Chuck Monts learned about mission in terms of compassion and others when he was eight years old. When his dad was a pastor, they had missionaries from Africa visit them. They were American Missionaries and then they would come back and raise more money to go back and do more mission work. Their eight-year-old daughter loved his Lite-Brite Set. He loved it himself. So they packed everything up and got ready to go.

Monts' dad was a man of few words, but he got his point across. He looked down and said, "I bet you that she would love the Lite-Brite set."

Monts looked up at him and said "What? Give her my Lite-Brite set?"

His dad didn't say anything more. He just sort of walked away. So, Monts wrapped up the chord and gave her the Lite-Brite Set. He says that it was very hard to do, but it was the right thing to do.

"I sort of learned about giving and service from my parents. They always did Christmas baskets and Thanksgiving baskets for little kids."

Monts, who was the former pastor at First Presbyterian Church in Hollidaysburg, set out on an adventure of a lifetime, when he biked from Los Angeles to New York City.

"I did it for the Bowery Mission. When you do something like this, there is a dimension of doing it for yourself. So, it's not just for the mission. I like adventure. You don't do something like this if you don't like adventure and you don't do something like this if you don't like physical challenge and I love physical challenge," he says.

Monts, who is almost sixty-two now, says that he gets crazy into physical challenge. He adds that when you're out there, you spend a lot of time on your bike. You have time to do an inventory and so you have time to discern where your growing areas are. He says that learning is part of it as well.

He says that what he learned about the most on this trip is that he actually lacks generosity and hospitality compared to what they experienced. "If I went back to this church or wherever I am going to be in the future, I now know that I can do a better job welcoming and serving people, who are asking for help and who are deserving and who aren't conning me."

Monts says that they had some try to con them, but they didn't get much from him, but the people who needed it, he says that he could have had a better or more generous attitude. He says that he can always improve in his life of serving others.

"So, I had to start from Los Angeles, which meant starting from a much hotter place in the country, then going to San Francisco. It meant that we had to go through the Mojave Desert, which meant dehydration issues and no cell reception. It was a learning curve for both my wife Debbie and me."

He says that you are allowed to take interstates in the west if they don't have a secondary paved road. So, he took 250 miles of interstates from Nevada to Utah. He does add that they are not that dangerous. "What I mean by that is today, I was on old Admiral Perry Highway. There were fewer cars, but a smaller shoulder. Who's to say which is more dangerous. Big shoulder and more cars going faster? For me, it wasn't unsafe. It was a little nerve-wracking and it was loud and it wasn't enjoyable. Then you pick up the little pieces of metal that fly off of radial tires when they break a part. It is better to get off of the interstate because of the metal, glass and stones."

Back in February, he started chopping up days fifty, sixty, seventy, eighty, ninety, 100, 120 was his longest day because towns were few and far between. He says that you either do a forty-mile day, which is ridiculous because you will never make it across the country in time or you do 120. Then, he adds, you have churches. "I made probably 350 phone calls before June 5th. Of all the churches, one in five would return my call. I don't think that is a good average for churches. There were five or six communities across the entire country that I did not have a church when I got there."

He continues, "One town that I biked in to, the pastor came home and lived right next to the church. I showed him my credentials and he said that the church elders have ruled that 'No one stays overnight in the church because we have a pre-school in there.'"

Monts says that for every community, pastor or church that said no, they had much more generosity, kindness, and over the top meals.

Monts on his journey across the country

His biggest challenge was being more patient with Debbie, because he was exhausted and impatient and stressed. It was very easy to fall into an impatient approach. He learned to instead of opening his mouth, say to himself, "Shut up for at least fifteen minutes." There was one day when he had expected that his wife had got to the church early and he thought that she might unload a little bit more than she did and I said, "I thought…never mind." That was better than finishing the sentence. "I still have room to grow."

Monts says that they had to do it together. "She wasn't going to work while I had the adventure of a lifetime. So, she did sightseeing for the most part. We were together every night and every morning. She had a good trip."

Monts believes a lot of people don't have big goals. They think about small goals. Most people wouldn't even think about biking across the country. It would not have even entered their mind. "I would say to a lot of people, Imagine doing something big. Just try to imagine it. What would it be? Doing a mission for a summer. Think of something and not just for yourself. So, imagine something big and imagine doing something big for someone else. That's a big push." He adds that most people are focused on themselves and are focused on what our culture tells us should be on our agenda, which is not really that big of a deal. "A car…I don't think that is a big thing. Maybe it is if you need transportation, but I mean in terms of accomplishments, in terms of meaning."

He continues, "Churches have the same problem. What big things are they thinking about today? Changing the carpet? They have been thinking of what they are doing for neighbors. That's big. Even if it's something small, its big. So, a food charity, hosting homeless families." Monts adds that the churches that said no to him, they are not thinking very big. They are thinking small. It's an inconvenience to have a stranger, even though they could verify who he was, it was an inconvenience. So, they are thinking small.

**Information for this article was obtained through an in-person interview with Chuck Monts
**Photos were provided by Chuck Monts

MARK PANEK

MARK PANEK

Legendary local drummer, Mark Panek, considers himself to be the Kevin Bacon of the Altoona music scene. He says, "Pick a band and go back ten steps, it comes back to me."

He has played with numerous area bands from Altoona and surrounding areas, including Pittsburgh and all over the state, basically. He earned his Master's in Music Business and Songwriting from Berklee College of Music in Boston. "Music has been a part of my life for my entire life."

His CDs can be downloaded from various sites from Spotify to Napster. One of his bands has their own channel on Pandora Radio entitled False Icons Radio. Their CD entitled God Complex was a worldwide release on Megaforce Records in 2008 and was featured in the motion picture, Wicked Lake in 2010.

While he currently resides in Tennessee, Panek has worked with a lot of nationally recognized artists such as Marshall Tucker, Lynyrd Skynyrd, Jo Dee Messina, Keith Urba,n and The Counting Crows. He counts among his close personal friends, Deborah Allen, who had a hit in 1983 with "Baby I lied" and Rikki Rockett from the 1980s hair band Poison.

He started out playing with his family's band Johnny Panek's Orchestra. He says that it was more or less like a Partridge Family type band. He adds that music in his family goes clear back to when his grandfather, Lakodia Panek, was abducted by gypsies and he had to play violin for his meàls in Poland. "Then, my dad and my uncles all played instruments, mostly horns. So, a lot of my childhood was playing music." He says, "I really didn't have a lot of good friends. Music was the thing that I have always played. That is the only thing that I knew, and it is the only thing that I will ever know."

In addition to being featured in an issue of Pennsylvania Musician, he has a full line of drum endorsements including with Sonor Drums, Vic Firth Drumsticks, DW Hardware, Latin Percussion, Audix Microphones, Attack Drumheads and Gibralter Racks. Sonor is the best on the market. They are handmade drums from Germany. I have a variety of drum sets including drumlines from their cheap line to their most expensive line. Panek recalls, "The drum industry loves my name. When I got endorsed by Rusty Martin from Sonor in 1988, they said, 'What a great name. It is very marketable.' They wanted to put an ad out with a slogan that would say 'Panek attack by Sonor.'"

Panek says that his biggest influence is Steve Smith from Journey. He is a very big reason that he plays Sonor Drums. "He has been a huge influence on my playing."

Touring all over the United States, Panek has done some opening spots with Jeff Healey as well as performing with Fat Vinny and The Wise Guys, which was a blues band. "I played with them in Texas and all over the west coast. We, even, had some interest from Blind Pig Records in San

Francisco. Through the course of time, he adds that there were some other bands he belonged to, who had potential. His band Toddo was almost signed to a division of MCA. Poverty Boys had interest from Atlantic Records and Tommy Gunn also had some interest from MCA.

Panek has also worked with country group Fred Myers and The Redneck Majority. They were signed to Tate Music Group. He was also with Pennsylvania's Chris Woodward, who was also a country artist.Through it all, he says that it has been one magical musical ride. Panek says the greatest achievement in his career has been obtaining his master's degree. "I was able through the grace of God to get that. He remembers that Rob Morgenstein, drummer for the eighties band Winger was his drum teacher.

He mentions that while growing up in Blair County, music had always been his mainstay. He says that it has always been his go to, and it was always there for him when he needed it to be. "If I was out of a job, I could always find a band to play in." Some of the bands that have considered him a valuable member include The Front, in the early nineties, Double Agents, Panek, The British Owls and Audio, among others. He says that he was even in four bands at once. Two of them were in Altoona and two of them were in Pittsburgh.

He later did some studio work in Stockton, CA. After that, he ended up venturing back little by little with stops in Chicago, Wisconsin, DC, and Florida. While in Florida, he played with a band called Martial Arts, which was a Sheraton band. They played the Sheraton Hotel Circuit.

"Music has always been my drive. It's always been my goal. It's always been my…you can do this. Actually, music has been my saving grace. As a kid, growing up, while most kids were getting high and driving fast and living dangerously, I was in my attic on 18th street, practicing drums. I loved it." He recalls, "As far as Blair County goes, it has been a steppingstone for me to other things."

He adds, that through the grace of God, his journey was able to continue after a head on collision in 1989. He reiterates that music has always been his saving grace. He says, "Me without music is like a car without wheels."

The advice that he would give to people from small town Pennsylvania that have goals that they want to achieve is to travel every avenue. Travel every road. You don't know who knows who. You don't know where that road will lead. Ninety-nine of them wind up going 120 mph into a brick wall, with no end, but still follow the road. It is not a race that is won for the swiftest. It is won by the one who gets stronger mile after grueling mile after setbacks, after disappointments after devastation after picking the pieces up and trying to assemble a career again. He says, "Do not quit. Don't let anyone deter you. Just keep going strong. Be quiet, watch and stay true to yourself."

**Information for this article was obtained through a phone interview with Mark Panek
**Photos are provided by Mark Panek

JACKIE RUSSO

JACKIE RUSSO

Beauty, Brains, and Heart (BBH)is a service organization that promotes positive pageantry with a purpose and encourages community service through volunteerism. Altoona native, Jackie Russo, along with her daughter Typhani founded the pageant-oriented service organization to give girls who are not the typical cookie cutter pageant person the opportunity to wear a sash and a crown and to learn about community volunteering and giving back and paying it forward in 2008.

"We want to reach out to young ladies who are more than just a pretty face! Those women who love competing in pageants but also are inspired through the pageant world to be involved in promoting their platform issues, are active in charitable organizations as well as within their community," Russo explains. "These girls are as beautiful on the inside as they are on the outside. They possess all of the necessary attributes to be positive role models and leaders. They are beautiful both physically and spiritually. They are intelligent, career-oriented, talented, virtuous, and compassionate! These girls who are so very comfortable being in the spotlight with their make-up, spray tans, beaded gowns and high-heeled shoes can be just as comfortable out of the limelight with a pair of jeans, a t-shirt and sneakers volunteering their time and talents. They are amazing young ladies who wear their crowns on their hearts."

Russo is also a former founder and director of Pennsylvania's Heart Inspired and Beautiful Pageant, Pennsylvania's Benevolent Jr Teen, Teen, Miss and Woman Pageant, Miss Holly Jolly Charity Pageant for Toys for Tots, Miss American Liberty Pageant, and the very fun Which Witch is Which Pageant.

BBH organizes an annual benefit Fashion Show. They have produced the Glam Across the Globe, Divas Through the Decades, Full Steam Ahead, and Pawsitively Purrfect Benefit Fashion Shows. With these events, they raised money to sponsor different charitable organizations. They also sponsored the annual fundraising dinner for Sideline Cancer, with money raised through Glam Across The Globe Fashion Show.

Russo last person standing in third row with the cast from "Glam Across the Globe" Fashion Show benefitting Sideline Cancer.

The Divas Through the Decades helped raise money for the American Cancer Society's Relay for Life. The Full Steam Ahead Fashion Show benefitted the prostate cancer organization. Through the Pawsitively Purrfect Benefit

Fashion Show, they collected food donations for the Central PA Humane Society as well as pajamas for the Pajama Program.

They have also produced and directed the 2012, 2013, 2014 and 2015 Pennsylvania USA Ambassador Pageants, and the 2008, 2009, 2010 and also the 2011 Pennsylvania's Perfect Jr Teen, Teen, Miss and Woman Pageant, and Pennsylvania's Little Miss Perfect Pageant.

They have partnered with local libraries to sponsor themed events such as a Storybook Ball, Hocus Pocus Bewitching Bash, and Spellbound Book Bonanza. They have donated their talents in partnership with the Mirror Moms for their Superhero Events and sponsored a TNT Talent Showcase Production. They work hands on with fundraising for many of the community charitable organizations and have collected new toys for eight years for Toys for Tots. They have also appeared on several reality shows and are available for judging.

Russo says that their first couple of title holders held the titles of Miss Benevolent Heart. These girls typically could not compete in pageants, because of the disability of wearing a brace or having some other health issue. "A lot of that has changed," Russo comments. "Back then, we wanted to give the girls, who wanted to do such things, but didn't have the opportunity and they were given the title of Miss Benevolent Heart." Since the inception of BBH, they have had twenty-eight young ladies who they have mentored.

Russo is also a former pageant director for ten years with two other systems having been the state director for Pennsylvania USA Ambassador for five years as well as the state director for Pennsylvania's Perfect Miss for five years. "I have mentored approximately forty queens over those ten years, many who have gone on to establish their own charity organizations and pageant systems. Many of them have also competed at higher levels of pageantry with one of my state queens going on to win the National title of that pageant and then went on to compete in the Miss America system and in 2020 was crowned Miss America."

Russo also has a young lady who she has mentored and was one of her Beauty, Brains, and Heart queens. She was an author and contributed her experiences in the book *I Fly*. In her story part of the book, it is about domestic violence. She mentioned Beauty, Brains, and Heart and how Russo had helped her through a rough time. That book was included in the celebrity bags at both the European version of The Emmys and at The Oscars as well. The woman has also started her own pageant system.

There are several former local queens who are still growing up and are still competing in other pageant systems and they do a lot of volunteering. "I have one little girl who I started in pageantry. She has her own community service organization at twelve years old. She was one of my state queens for a system that I directed when she was only four."

When asked about how she got the organization started,

she says that her daughter has been involved with pageantry since she was a baby and Russo, herself, has been volunteering and doing community service the majority of her life since she was a teenager. The two go hand in hand. "I thought that it would help the two of us maintain our close relationship and allow us to have our mother-daughter bonding if we did something that both of us enjoyed while helping others at the same time. So, that is basically why we started Beauty, Brains, and Heart."

Russo (2nd from left) with her daughter Typhani (third from the right) and their team for the American Cancer Society's Relay for Life Event.

As far as the future goes, "We are going to continue to do what we do. We have our themed activities, and we are always organizing different events throughout the community to help raise money and sponsor various organizations if we are able to."

Russo says that they also sponsor two awards. They have

a Benevelont Heart award that she donates to different pageant systems that they in turn award to a contestant who goes above and beyond in their own community. She adds that she and Typhani also recently started a Community Superhero Award. "Our team queens—we call them superheroes with crowns. So, we have started a Community Superhero Award that we give out. We have given out three of those so far. The first one was presented to Greenbean Coffeehouse and the second one was given to K.C. O'Day and the third went to The Mountain Lion BackPack Program. The award is for their volunteerism, involvement and all that they do, going above and beyond in the community and giving back and paying it forward."

They also publish a magazine four times a year called *BBH Magazine*. They feature pageant contestants in their superheroes with crowns pages and they also spotlight different reigning titleholders and talk about their title, platform issues and what they are involved in.

The advice that she would give to people from small town Pennsylvania that have goals that they want to achieve is, "You have the ability and capability to do anything that you want to do. If you have the heart's desire to do something just do it." She also says, "Always remember to be yourself."

Russo was also one of the four finalists for the Remarkable Women of Central Pennsylvania and was Director of the Year for the USA Ambassador Pageant System. "I just do my thing without expecting any kind of recognition. I do it just because I enjoy it and it helps to build the bond between my daughter and me and we like mentoring young ladies and helping them move forward with their dreams and aspirations."

Beauty, Brains, and Heart's mission statement is promoting positive pageantry with a purpose and encouraging community service through volunteerism. Russo stresses the importance of the pageant's motto, "Remember you are a beauty using your brains to guide your compassionate heart."

**Information for this article was obtained through an in-person interview with Jackie Russo
**Photos were provided by Jackie Russo

JACK SERVELLO

JACK SERVELLO

Jack Servello has been involved with music in the Altoona area since 1980. He started out in a band called The Midnight Skies with Charlie Shannon. He began playing with them in 1980 after he graduated high school. He played places like The Knotty Pine in East Freedom and the Altoona fraternal clubs and things like that. He played with them until 1982.

They were playing at The Brass Rail for country night. "I had seen in the paper that The Spoon River Band, which was a big country band in the area at the time, was looking for a guitar player. I didn't think that I was good enough for that band." He was just twenty years old. "We were playing at The Brass Rail and I am looking out and saw Dennie Huber talking with my parents. I go on break and my dad says Dennie wants to introduce you to somebody."

Dennie introduced Jack to Mark Snyder and Craig Shaffer of The Spoon River Band. He talked with them and they asked him to come and audition. "The other members of the band were also there. We did one song, 'Cryin' My Heart Out Over You.'"

The band sang the chorus and Jack sang the high part. Servello says, "They stopped and started laughing. I asked them what they were laughing about. They said that it took them six months to teach the other guy how to sing that part. I got it on the first try. I was with The Spoon River

Band for two years." He played on their second LP. He also wrote a song on that record as well. They played everywhere including festivals and fairs. They also played in Montoursville for cookie days. That is where they make Archway Cookies. The biggest show that they did was opening for Conway Twitty at The Cambria County Fair in 1983 in front of about four thousand people.

After Spoon River, he joined a band called The Prime Time Band, which played oldies. "I played with them for twenty some years." They had prime time parties that they did for their fans, once a year, which included a floor show.

In addition to those bands, Servello had a band of his own called The Organized Sound with his brother and his brother's friend. They played at Lakemont Park and things like that. They also performed as The Servello Family. Under that name, they were the first band to ever play at Heritage Plaza in downtown Altoona, at the dedication of the plaza. They played at Boyertown USA as well. "We were the only group to get paid by Boyertown after we performed."

Jack also writes commercial jingles such as the J&P Auto Mart jingle. He wrote "Here Comes Steamer" for The Altoona Curve which they play at every game. As he was preparing to take the song to them, his friend Cory Geishauser, who played Steamer, called and said that they want to hear the theme song that you wrote for the Curve, too. Servello ended up writing "Let's Hear it for the Curve", which the Curve bought but never used. Rich Dileo, who is still on the radio, sometimes plays "Let's Hear it for the Curve" on his sports program.

Servello said, "The Prime Time Band recorded a single, which I wrote called 'I want to love you'. I took a copy up to WALY 104 where Steve Willett and Debbie Hoy were doing their morning show. They invited me up and put me on the air and played the song, sound unheard. They just put it on the turntable and played it."

Servello, who has been writing songs since he was sixteen years old, has a recording studio in his house. He has been recording since 1994. He started out with a four track cassette and now he has unlimited tracks. He can do any kind of instrument that you want. He has a guitar that he runs through a synthesizer that allows him to play all kinds of different sounds.

His son Richard Servello plays drums for him on those songs. He records them at his house and then sends them to his dad. Then, Jack puts them on the song and gets it done as fast as he can. He says that he has recorded over five thousand tracks since 1994.

Servello proudly says, "On any given Sunday, my music could be playing at a hundred different places because of all of the people who we have recorded Gospel tracks for." He said he would be surprised some times when he will be listening to local Christian radio and a local group comes on and it is their music playing.

Jack was looking for the words to the song "Simon Says" by the 1910 Fruitgum Company, because he wanted to include it in what The Servello Family does. About fifteen or twenty years ago, he visited the group's website, and sent them a message. They responded. Long story short, Jack got to be on-line friends with the current lead singer Mick Mansuetto. Eventually, they were given a chance to have five of their songs put on a compilation CD of bubblegum music. They only had four songs that they could use and they needed a fifth one. The song that they wanted to add was "Goody Goody Gumdrops". The group wanted Jack to make a track for them because they didn't have time to go into the studio.

"I got the record from my mom and I duplicated the song exactly from what was on the record and I sent it to them. Frank Jeckell, who started the band, sent me an email saying that he was skeptical when Mick said that he had me do this track. He said that I nailed it." So, the band put their vocals on that track and the song appears on the compilation CD that people can buy. Nobody knows that it is not them playing.

"It's little things like that, that I have done that nobody knows about. I don't go bragging, 'Look what I have done.' Some people get noticed more than others and that's okay. It's not a big deal. I know what I can do and I keep doing it just because that's what I do." Servello says.

Dr. Demento has played several of his and his partner Bill Dann's songs over the years. Dann, who writes the lyrics, is a poet. Servello turns these poems into songs.

Jack says that Dann sends out emails and people get right back to him. For instance, they did a radio program for Halloween about four years ago called The Haunted Jukebox. Bill sent a message to Butch Patrick, who played Eddie Munster on The Munsters. He got right back to Bill and said that he would come. He cohosted the thing. They recorded it at Servello's mom and dad's place on their front porch in 2016. "Butch Patrick was on my parent's front porch and we recorded the dialogue for this program. Then, I edited everything together. We created a three and a half hour radio program."

They have talked to people like Ron Dante from The Archies. They have talked to Fred Vail, The Beach Boys' original manager, when they were younger and just out of school as well as with Peter Noone from Herman's Hermits.

They had a song that made national television. The program, Paranormal Paparazzi, however, wasn't picked up. The song was, "Thor, the Purple Squirrel from Jersey Shore". The show was looking for Big Foot in Jersey Shore, PA. They heard about the purple squrrel. Servello says that Pee Wee Herman shared this story from Accu-Weather about this squirrel that people captured in Jersey Shore that was purple. Bill wrote a song about it. It has over 25,000 views on YouTube because it was on national television.

As far as the future goes, Servello syas, "We are going to keep doing what we are doing and hope that we can get somewhere with it. At some point, we have to write something that stands out." For Servello, a song that stands out is "Heroes Close to Home", which Bill wrote in honor of a guy from Bellefonte. His unit was hit by an explosive device. They got permission to have this man in the video. Blair County native New York photographer Nick Finochio shot the video. It was mostly shot in Bellefonte, with part of it being shot in downtown Altoona at the veterans mall. Servello thinks that that song should have 25,000 views. "I sent it to Gary Sinise, who is big with the veterans. They do the Memorial Day Parade in Washington. We went down with the high school band when my son was with them. Gary Sinise and all of these famous people were down there as the parade marshals. I sent the song to them but I don't seem to make the contact. It is really difficult to make that contact."

Talking about growinng up in Altoona, Servello says that, without sounding too derogatory, Altoona is a sports town. He says that if you throw a football, even remotely well, you're going to get attention and if you play someone a song, it's like, "Oh, okay".

"I love the small town that I was born in." In 1999, it was Altoona's sesquicentennial and he wrote the official sesquicentennial song for the city. It was titled "Altoona is My Home". He is on YouTube, singing the song at the Altoona Alliance Church for the Sesquicentennial Worship Service that they had. He said that he saw the ad in the paper, he went down, had the song and made some CDs and it didn't go well. Long story short, they were at the Jaffa Shrine Center for the sesquicentennial concert. "I was not part of it. I was not included in the concert to do the song. Why? I don't know. Paul Winter was involved. Mike Reid was involved. I played my song out on the portico as people were going into the Jaffa. I didn't even have tickets. Someone came out and gave us tickets. We were up in the last row in peanut heaven. We did get invited downstairs to the basement for the after concert meet and greet. Paul Winter came up to me and said, 'If I had your song nine months ago, you would have been in the show.'"

Servello told Paul that he had given his song through the proper channels to get it to him and they didn't forward it to him. He adds, "There was a lost opportunity." He says that maybe he is too forgiving but he thinks that he is supposed to be. He adds that it doesn't matter now. "It is many years later. I am still doing what I am doing. It didn't take anything away from me."

His advice to someone from small town Pennsylvania who have big goals is, "I don't think that you can do it from small town Altoona. You have to go where the people are, who can get you where you need to be. Never take for granted where you came from. Go where the people are. Go where the action is. Always remember that when you achieve your success, don't forget your hometown. Paul Winter never forgets his hometown. Mike Reid never forgets his hometown. I respect both of those guys, just for the fact that they made it big, but they never forgot where they came from. Their hearts are really in Altoona. So is mine. Altoona is my home. Go for your dreams but remember where you came from. Keep that close to your heart.

**Information for this article was obtained through a phone interview with Jack Servello

**Photos were provided by Jack Servello

JOE SERVELLO

JOE SERVELLO

Altoona native, artist, and illustrator Joe Servello continues doing the work that he loves so much. He is currently working on a book called *Senor Frog*.

Servello began his life after high school graduation, working in the shops for about six months before joining the Navy, during the Korean War. After the Navy, he went to Penn State and graduated with a degree in Art Education. He later worked at Penn State in television and graphics. A couple of years later, he went to New York City to be in an Off-Broadway play called The World of Gunter Grass, followed by working in theater in Buffalo as an actor for about two or three years. After that, he went back to New York City. Servello says that all of this time, he was always drawing and was interested in illustrating books, illustrating anything. "I was always working. I did the posters for the theater."

When he got back to New York, he reconnected up with his old friend from college, William Kotzwinkle and put together a children's book, which he took around to different publishers. Finally, it was accepted and printed. That was their first book. It was called *The Fireman*. It was about a little boy who got a toy fire truck.

They worked on other books, together, mostly children's books. "We worked together in the city until he left and then we worked by mail together." They did about twenty different books together including books for adults and other kinds of projects.

Servello moved back to Altoona in 1986. He continued to illustrate, working with authors by mail and shpping stuff back and forth to publishers. Over the years, he had some exhibits, including exhibits in group shows in New York City. He also worked on murals including one in a theater on Long Island and a hospital in New York.

He has also done murals, locally since coming back to Altoona. He has had a couple of exhibits at the Altoona Campus, as well and continues illustrating up until this day. He also taught illustration at the Altoona Campus for a couple of years.

Servello says that it is hard to say what initially sparked his interest in art, because he has always been interested. "As a child, I used to love the comic strips and they of course were done by very good artists in those days." He started drawing when he was very young.

Both of his parents encouraged him to stay interested in art. Servello said he loved growing up here because he found that everybody was very encouraging. His teachers in grade school and high school were very encouraging. He mentions Ruby Crum, a wonderful teacher, commissioned him to do some things even while he was still in high school.

He says that he always loved books and was always reading. When he went to Penn State, he had the greatest teacher that he ever had by the name of Edwin Zoler. He would give him more books to read. "I would always have a library book out. We have a great library here. So, I really took advantage of that." He says that he liked a lot of the comic strip artists influenced her work as well. He liked N.C. Wyeth a lot.

Servello found that Blair County was very encouraging for artists. He adds that not that there is very much money being spent on buying pictures or anything like that. "It is a very positive thing around here."

He spent an afternoon showing his work to Maurice Sendak. He was very encouraging. He was his favorite children's book artist and writer. "He was very helpful and sent me to his editor and I did a book with the editor."

He adds that the other artist was also very helpful. He did a very famous book called *Snowy Day*. He took Servello to his editor and introduced him and was very helpful.

"Those were the two artists who were the most help to me and were sort of my mentors," Servello remembers.

Servello has lost count of how many books that he has done, but says that it is certainly at least forty-five books, maybe more. With those, some were children's books and some were where he did just one or two illustrations and some were picture books. He also did a lot of work for magazines including *Cricket*, an artistic magazine for children.

Then, he did a whole lot of covers for a publisher who published old detective stories. He did about twenty or more of those book jackets.

His best advice to those, living in small town Pennsylvania who have big goals is to never give up. "You have to get used to being rejected when you go into the arts." He says you have to try to learn something from rejection and you have to keep learning as much as you can and never give up. He adds that these days because of the internet, you never have to leave a small town.

"When I started, all of the publishing was done in New York. When I went to New York and went from publisher to publisher, getting rejected, I would learn something new every time." In those days, he says, you could just call up and make an appointment with the art director of a big publisher. He says that you can't do that anymore. You have to send things over the internet or drop off your portfolio. You don't get to talk to these people. "You don't get to learn as much."

"I think being an artist is a very satisfying profession. It is a little harder than people think but at the same time, you have control over what you're doing. You can work your own hours." He doesn't think being an artist pays very much money, but it is worth it in many other ways. "People are very kind and appreciate your work and pat you on the back. That's all very nice but the actual work is what I mostly enjoy."

His final word of advice is, "If you pick a profession that you really like, it is not like work at all. You just enjoy your job so much, it's like you don't have a job."

**Information for this article was obtained through a phone interview with Joe Servello
**Photo was provided by Joe Servello.

MEGHAN SINISI

MEGHAN SINISI

Altoona native, Meghan Sinisi, says that the Miss America Organization hasn't always been a part of her journey. She discovered this in college, and it was a venue to combine her different interests.

The 2013 Altoona Area High School graduate, who was recently crowned Miss Pennsylvania, has been twirling baton since she was three years old. It was her main extracurricular activity throughout her childhood going into college.

After being selected Homecoming Queen in high school, she decided she wanted to do something meaningful with it. Her aunt worked in the Special Education department. She asked her aunt if she could visit her life skills class. "My aunt said, 'Yes, of course. The students would love to see you in your sash and crown.' So, I visited the classroom. That was the first time that I had interacted with somebody who had autism and I realized how little we were taught about the actual people behind the label of autism. It is a word that is thrown around a lot."

During Autism Awareness Month, a lot of people hear about autism, but not many people consider what it means to live with it. After talking with the students, she realized how they needed a champion in their corner. They have things that they can accomplish and contribute to society, and they deserve that. They deserve that type of independence and people to believe in them. "That is what really sparked my interest in doing something in my career to help people with autism. That eventually led me to select speech pathology as my career. Then, it helped me discover the Miss America Organization as well."

She had a passion for advocating for the autism community, which eventually led into a career path in speech pathology. When she discovered the Miss America Organization, she tied that together with her baton twirling.

In addition to those, she was a student at Syracuse University, and she was not currently receiving a scholarship to attend. "The Miss America Organization was a culmination of all of the things that I was looking to pursue as a young woman."

Sinisi has competed for about six years, since 2015. This was her final year of competition eligibility. Now, she will be representing Altoona and Pennsylvania on the Miss America stage for the 100th anniversary of the competition.

She remembers what it was like winning the title. "It was a surreal moment. I had been working toward this for quite some time and you work so hard, and you put in all of that dedication toward something but you're not sure what the outcome might be." Sinisi continued with, "In the moment of being called Miss Pennsylvania, I was very grateful just to be in the final two and to share that moment with my first runner up and at that time, I was very pleased with my performances, and I was ready to step into the role as Miss

Pennsylvania and I knew that I had put in all of the work necessary. I was very excited about the opportunity to make a difference. I thought that I would be a very good representative of Pennsylvania."

She was excited, but they actually called the first runner's-up name first and they had been told that going into it. She had to remind herself that it wasn't the winner's name. It was the first runner's up name. "It took me a second to even realize that it was my name being called as Miss Pennsylvania. From there, I was just on cloud nine and so happy and thrilled for the journey ahead."

Sinisi remembers walking across the stage waving to the audience and then she had the chance to stand right in the center and scan across the audience and look for her family and look toward the judges who helped to select her. That was the first moment in all of the excitement that she got to soak it all in.

Immediately afterward, her class of sisters ran up and gave her a hug. She says that it was really great to see all of that support from the class of women who she gets to represent for the next year.

Her social impact initiative is dedicated to inspiring Autism Acceptance. "This is a project that I have been working on for quite some time since my senior year in high school. In May 2020, I adopted this initiative into a non-profit organization, which is called 'From a New Perspective'. So, through my advocacy work as Miss Pennsylvania, and as a non-profit founder and President, I hope to challenge misconceptions about autism and then help families and children with autism be connected with resources in their community. That way, they can reach their highest level of success.

"My main priority as Miss Pennsylvania is breaking down those stereotypes and helping people without autism or without disabilities understand that people with autism are people too and they deserve a place in our society, and they deserve to have independence and work toward their goals without unnecessary barriers in their way."

Sinisi adds, as Miss Pennsylvania, she will work with legislators to ensure that people with autism and disabilities have rights and access to different opportunities that are typically given to those without disabilities. Then, as Miss America, she would hope to expand this, not, just in Pennsylvania but across all fifty states and bring it as far and wide as possible, so, as many families as possible can have the resources that they need to be successful.

When thinking about the stereotypes associated with pageantry, Sinisi believes it very important to point out that the Miss America Organization has been challenging those stereotypes against women ever since its inception. "This kind of feeds into the current stereotype that pageants are all about beauty. At one time, it was about being a bathing beauty on the Atlantic City boardwalk. In our history, in 1921, when this started, that was very pivotal for a woman to parade the boardwalk in a swimsuit. So, we were breaking barriers and challenging what it meant to be a woman all the way back in the 1920s.

"Since that is what we started as…a beauty competition…that is what sometimes, people still think of when they think of Miss America. People don't realize that we are also very successful women in our careers. We are ambitious and we are smart, and we are passionate about creating change for the people around us and I will say that's the biggest misconception or stereotype. It presents the most challenge. We are constantly having to defend our place and because there is a little bit of glamour of being Miss Pennsylvania and Miss America. A lot of times, when we walk into the boardroom or a corporate office, we have to always be on our game and almost have to prove our worth to be there."

Sinisi says that in the past few years, especially, the Miss America Organization decided to nix the swimsuit competition. The reason behind that was to focus more on what a woman has to say and the impact that she has than her appearance.

"We're entering a whole new era of Miss America and what it means to be a businesswoman and a non-profit founder and lawyer. Miss America can be all of those things."

She sums it up by saying that those are some of the stereotypes that are challenging to us, but the direction that they are going is very positive in her opinion. It allows them to reach more people and to get people invested in the missions that they stand for.

Miss Pennsylvania and Miss America was not always on Sinisi's radar, but she does say that in Altoona, her family comes from Italy. Her grandparents were first generation Americans, and they grew up very young in America. Their parents had the American Dream. For them, that was coming to America and working on the Pennsylvania Railroad.

"They had to work very hard for the life that they lived.

They thought that it was the dream that they always wanted. That hard work ethic and that integrity that they built from the time that they came here trickled down through generations and was instilled in me as well," Sinisi said. "That's what I love about Altoona. We have so many different cultures in Blair County, and we come from many different places. Much of that is because of The Industrial Revolution. The Pennsylvania Railroad was right there as well. I would not be the woman that I am today without each and every person who contributed to raising me."

Sinisi's hard work ethic was instilled in her by her parents. They had always encouraged her to reach higher and to always dream big and never let the naysayers get you down. Of course, throughout anybody's life, people are told a lot of times what they can and cannot do, but the only person that can dictate your future is yourself. "So, anytime that I hadn't accomplished anything that I wanted, I went after an even greater ambition after that."

She continues that baton twirling was a very large part of her childhood. She attributes a lot of her success to her coaches and athletes who she looked up to as a little girl. They really helped her to dream and let her know that she can accomplish great things as well, because they had done it. She says, that if she can be just as great of a role model for people, she will feel really successful no matter what happens at Miss America. "Of course, my family...they have always believed in me. They have been those people in my corner who, when I didn't believe in myself, they reminded me why I was working so hard toward my accomplishments and my endeavors."

She grew up with three brothers. So, pageantry wasn't the typical thing that was in their family. She says that it has been great to have those brothers. They always protected her and always wanted to make sure that they had her back throughout her life. "Now, it feels really good to be a representative. They seem really proud as well. To have them on this journey has been really special."

Sinisi adds "When I discovered The Miss America Organization, it seemed like the pinnacle of what I wanted to accomplish as a young woman…to be a role model for other young women, to have a successful career, and to earn scholarships for my education."

She says that coming from a middle-class family…for college, she had to really look for some resources to make it more affordable for her. That is why coming to the Miss America Organization was very enticing, in order to make her education more affordable.

The advice that she would give to people who have big goals to accomplish is to encourage them and tell them that she once felt that way intuitively. However, she always set the bar higher for herself. She says that a goal seems lofty when you first set it, but you take small steps every day toward something that you truly want. If it is something that is in your heart, you can accomplish it. She says that she is living proof of it. She left Altoona to pursue her education. She went to Syracuse University. Then, she came back home and then got her master's degree at the University of Missouri.

She continues by saying that each time that she left to achieve something greater, she had that inner want to come back home and to bring all of what she learned from other places, including the diversity that she had seen, so that she could hopefully instill that in others as well.

"Go for your dreams. Never stop dreaming. Whenever you accomplish one thing, no matter how big or small, set the bar even higher for yourself and don't stop until you get there. Know that no one can dictate your dreams for you. So, continuously work toward whatever it is that you see as success for yourself." Sinisi continues, "A lot of times, throughout my life, that involved me being my own biggest cheerleader. Sometimes that is necessary for people to know that sometimes you won't have a lot of people in your corner but if you can encourage yourself and keep going, you can certainly achieve anything that you set your mind to, even if you are from small town Altoona."

As far as the future goes, Sinisi says if she would have the opportunity to be Miss America, she would serve as a national ambassador for their program and partner with the organization to be a representative of their brand. "If I am not fortunate enough to become Miss America, it is actually wonderful that I get to come home and be Miss Pennsylvania for the remainder of my year. So, I will continue to advocate for my social impact initiative which is autism acceptance from a new perspective."

Sinisi would love to leave a legacy that means bringing as many Pennsylvanians into this journey as possible and hoping to reach many different areas across the state that had never had the opportunity to meet a Miss Pennsylvania. She hopes to reach far and wide across Pennsylvania and especially to recognize the people who helped to make this organization what it is, including our local volunteers and directors and to really honor them for their commitment to really making a program that is so wonderful for young women to achieve greatness.

Next June, she will crown her successor, Miss Pennsylvania 2022. "Then, I will enter a career in speech pathology and hopefully work with early intervention or children with disabilities, specifically autism."

Her long-term goals include to own and operate her own comprehensive therapy clinic for children with disabilities. "I would bring my expertise as a speech pathologist and hopefully work with a pediatrician or psychologist and people within the medical and health professions to serve the autism community and the disability community."

In the meantime, Sinisi continues to prep for The Miss America Competition by working with her team within the Miss PA Scholarship Foundation to prepare for interviews. "Part of the competition is a ten-minute interview with the judges. You can be asked anything and everything under the sun. I will be preparing myself to answer hard hot topic political questions, information about myself and about my goals as Miss America and something that is very important to me, which is continuously staying authentic and true to myself…always striving to improve, but at the root, keeping my foundation of who I am as Meghan Sinisi going into Miss America. I will also be practicing my talent. So, I will get to perform my baton twirling on The Miss America stage. We will get to walk in evening gown. I will be selecting my wardrobe as well."

She finished with, "I will, also, be talking about my social impact initiative. We have something called a social impact pitch. However, I think the biggest part of preparation within the next few months is interacting face to face with different people in the community. That's the best type of preparation…to walk into a room with people from different backgrounds and be able to connect with them. I hope to interact with as many community members and organizations to understand what it is that Pennsylvania wants in a national representative and then what the country would want in their Miss America as well."

**Information for this article was obtained through a phone interview with Meghan Sinisi
**Photos were provided by Meghan Sinisi and the Miss Pennsylvania Scholarship Foundation Inc.

JAKE SNYDER

JAKE SNYDER

Even at a young age, Altoona native, Jake Snyder, was already showing his musical abilities. He taught himself to play the piano. His father had wanted him to play the accordion, which was a heavy instrument for his small size and age, so his mother would put the accordion into a red wagon and pull it across town to his music lesson.

His wife Cheryl, who he married in 1974, says that she remembers Jake in ninth grade, being a vocalist at Keith Junior High school. She remembers him singing at special assemblies and things like that.

Piano playing came naturally to him. He had a gift where he could hear a song and then he could play it. Cheryl says that his whole being was in tune to music. She adds that it was his lifeblood. She remembers that music was probably the most important aspect of his life, except for his faith and family.

Graduating from Altoona Area High School in 1967, Snyder attended Penn State University, Altoona Campus from 1967 to 1969 and then attended the main campus in State College from 1969 to 1971, graduating in 1971 with a Bachelor of Science in secondary school music education. He also received from Penn State, his Master of Music Education in 1975, a Professional certificate as Secondary Principal in 1993 and Professional Certificate as Superintendent in 1995. Then, he went on to earn a master's degree in Ministry from Grace Theological Seminary in 2000.

He and his wife went on to have two sons, Jason and Justin. Justin and his wife, then blessed them with three lovely granddaughters. In 1983, Jason was diagnosed with leukemia and after several months of chemotherapy, went into remission. However, he relapsed almost a year later and passed away in 1984.

This was a difficult time for the family, but Jake and Cheryl put their trust in God to guide them. With God as their anchor and family and friends as their support, they were able to have peace during this time and the years afterward.

Following Snyder's graduation from Penn State, he got the job that he wanted all along. He was hired as music teacher and choral director at Keith Junior High School from 1971 to 1976. In 1976, he was moved to the music teacher/choral director position at Altoona Area High School after his high school music director had retired. Snyder worked there until 1990. From 1990 to 1997, he worked at Tussey Mountain High School as the junior/senior high school principal. Then, from 1997 to 2003, he worked at Penn Cambria High School as principal. He retired in 2003. During those years, he worked at various times at Penn State Altoona teaching several different music courses and later, some religion courses. Overall, Snyder loved teaching and loved working with children and teens of all ages, encouraging and inspiring them. He also taught private lessons in guitar, voice, and piano—early in his career and later after retirement.

He enjoyed making things fun and interesting for the kids who he worked with. At Tussey Mountain, to encourage the reading teacher, he challenged every seventh-grade student (ninety in all) to read a book on animals during the third marking period and do a subsequent project on their chosen animal. How did he do this? He promised to kiss a pig. He kissed Sebastian the pig.

While at Penn Cambria, students were encouraged to have a fundraiser for the local Relay for Life, raising over $2,000. They sent him to jail. Snyder had agreed to spend one hour for each $100 raised, in solitary confinement at the Cambria County prison. He did just that. The police took him away in handcuffs and gave him a new orange outfit.

Jake loved working with kids of any age. He loved, not

just teaching them music, but encouraging and supporting them. He would be one of the few teachers and then as principal, and often interacted with special needs children. He loved every child and there have been different kids through the years, who have said how much of an impact that Snyder had on their lives and how he had changed their lives.

Snyder also had a very nice semi-professional music career. He joined the Vicksburg Quartet in 1969 and was with them for a total of thirty years. He was lead singer along with playing the guitar and accordion. He tied this in with his faith. When they would perform at churches, sometimes he would be asked to give a brief message.

He worked both of those things into his life…his love for music and entertaining and his desire to serve God. Cheryl says that she knows that after he became a father, he did miss being at home. Occasionally, he had opportunities to take one of their sons with him. Those were special moments.

She remembers when they spent four or five days in Lancaster at Dutch Wonderland. The Vicksburgs were singing there. Two of the guys took their sons. It was just a good father-son time.

At one time, everybody in the group was a teacher. So, they all had the summers off. That is when they would perform at the fairs and festivals. During the rest of the year, they would play mostly Saturdays and Sundays. They all had the same schedule for a few years. It worked out perfectly.

In the late 1970s, when he was not with the Vicksburgs, he started a contemporary Christian music group, The Morning Light, which sang in churches throughout the area for several years. They were the opening act one time at the Jaffa Mosque for B.J. Thomas.

Later, in 2006, he sang in a country Gospel group, called The Snyder Brothers and Schaffer, with his brother Mark and a friend, Craig Schaffer.

Snyder also operated a recording studio on location at first, before building a studio attached to his home. He began in 1980, recording more than a hundred albums (LPs, cassettes and then CDs). He also performed soundtracks for clients, recorded single demos and even worked on an advertising jingle or two. This is just to name a few things he did. His last project was doing a recording of the Bible (beginning to end) for an international organization. Those who read the Bible were all local people approved by the organization. This was an extremely fulfilling and impactful end to his recording career. He was doing this through early 2015, when his cancer made it too hard for him to continue.

His music was in every facet of his life. His career as an educator was music related. His semi-professional career was music. He taught private lessons. He was a music director at his church, and he was always willing to do special music at church as well. "Music was his lifeblood."

Snyder served in every church that he and his wife attended. He was licensed by the Association of Grace Brethren Churches in 2004 as a licensed minister. Several years later, he was then ordained. He helped plant a Grace Brethren Church in Saxton, serving as the pastor. In the Martinsburg Grace Brethren Church, he served as the Minister of Music and also taught a Sunday School class and preached when needed. He served as an interim pastor for Pike Grace Brethren Church in Johnstown while they were searching for a new pastor. At Leamersville Grace Brethren Church, he assisted the pastor, "filling the pulpit" on occasion and helped with the praise team.

Snyder on a mission trip to Jos, Nigeria (Africa)

He also served on mission trips with the first one being in 1996 to Novosibirsk, Siberia, Russia, with a team from Martinsburg Grace Brethren Church. Then in 2003, he went to Prague, Czech Republic, also with a team from Martins-burg Grace Brethren Church. In 2008, he went to Jos, Ni-geria, Africa with the Leamersville Grace Brethren Church pastor and a group from a Grace Brethren Church near Philadelphia. These trips were life-changing experiences for him.

Cheryl says that Jake grew up in a Christian home and in a middle-class family. He didn't have money or prestige be-hind him, but he had the love and support of his family.

While growing up in the Altoona Area School District, he was encouraged by his teachers. He was thrilled when he finally finished his education, and he got the job of his dreams at Keith Junior high School.

Cheryl says that as far as advice goes, Jake was such an encourager of the youth. He had a big impact on a lot of his students' lives. He would believe that it is not where you come from but who you are. "We all have God-given abili-ties that we can do whatever we set our minds to."

In 1995, Jake was diagnosed with metastatic squamous cell carcinoma of the neck. He had two surgeries and weeks of radiation, but he was call cured several years later. This was a rough time for him, but he kept going and went to work, leaving early for radiation. Despite the radiation burns and fatigue, he sided his house that summer. It took a bit longer, due to the breaks that he needed, but it got done with some help from a friend.

In 2012, the cancer returned. With what is called stereo-tactic radiosurgery (intense radiation pinpointing the tumor only) and some chemo, it seemed to be gone. However, in December of 2013, there was another "hot spot" and he had a lymph node removed.

With 2014 being a good year, clean PET scans and MRIs, the cancer returned in 2015. An excision of a malignant neoplasm of the hypopharynx was performed with radiation and chemotherapy following. However, another diagnosis of CA of mediastinum. Again, stereotactic radiation and chemotherapy. Another new area in the neck plus a lymph node in the lung showed cancer. They tried immunotherapy which was being tested for recurring head/neck cancer. This didn't work either and the Snyders were told in March of 2016 that they really couldn't do any more. Because of breathing difficulties, he had a tracheostomy done in April of 2016. Jake went Home to be with his Heavenly Father in August of 2016.

**Information for this article was obtained through an interview with Cheryl Snyder
**Photos were provided by Cheryl Snyder

THE WALTERS AND THE DUNCAN FAMILY

Jacob Walters homestead

THE WALTERS FAMILY AND THE DUNCAN FAMILY

Along old Route 22 in the middle of Duncansville, PA is the first structure built in the borough. The log cabin was built circa 1820.

The Walters family settled in the area before the canal days, which began in the early 1830's. They came out of Lancaster County as many families did and traveled west through Pennsylvania. Route 22 was one of the earliest routes coming from the east. Coming out of Harrisburg, Route 22 was a Native American path which followed the Juniata River.

Along this route, the little towns, along the river, are about fifteen miles apart. The average travel for a Conestoga wagon coming west was about fifteen miles a day. They would stop every fifteen miles until they would reach their destination.

The reason that Duncansville was an early settlement was because as families were coming west in the early 1800s, this was still Indian country. They didn't settle here until they felt that the Native Americans had moved westward.

Legend has it that as the wagons came west into the area, they saw the mountains up ahead and said that this was as far as they were going. That is why the Walters family settled here. They ended up building several log cabins in the immediate area. The lone remaining cabin was the largest one.

The Walters family settled on the east side of the Blair River and then The Duncan family had settled on the west side of the river. As a result, you had Walterstown on the east side and Duncansville on the west side of the river.

In the early 1830s the canal started ending in Hollidaysburg. As more and more people were moving in, building homes, and settling, they decided to rename the area one name. Legend has it that both the Walters family and the Duncan family met at the bridge in Duncansville. They flipped a coin. Heads it would be Duncansville and tails it would be Walterstown. It came up heads. So, the town has been known as Duncansville since 1836.

Samuel Duncan ~ Margaret McNamara Duncan
1783~1864   1793~1865
Founder of Duncansville ~ 1831

The Duncans

According to local historian, Dave Czuba, the Walters family is not very well known. He says that they had close to twelve children, which is why the cabin was so large. There is a Walters family cemetery, which has approximately forty to fifty graves, above Duncansville, about a half mile up on the hill. However, over the course of a couple of hundred years, they have been mostly weather beaten. Somewhere in the history books, there are the names of those buried up there.

Czuba says, as far as what the family did for a living, it is not known for sure. "I have never been lucky enough to find a ledger or a diary or some sort of handwritten account of just exactly how many businesses or homes were in Walterstown. The best guess is that there were forty to fifty buildings."

Czuba remembers, to the best of his knowledge, four other log cabins still stand in the borough. He said that they are currently sided over. He says that this one was also sided over and had paneling on the inside. Everything was covered over two or three times. He says that the people that were living here did not even know that it was a log cabin.

On the other side of the river, Samuel Duncan was part of the iron and nail business on the west side of town where the Antique Depot currently sits.

There was no real rivalry between the two families. However, Czuba says that the Walters were definitely disappointed that they lost the coin toss.

**Portions of this article were originally written by Eric Shields for the Morrison Cove Herald and Hollidaysburg Herald newspapers in November 2020
**Information for this article was obtained through an in-person interview with Dave Czuba
**Photos were taken by Eric Shields

CPL DON WESTLEY

CPL. DONALD L WESTLEY

CPL Donald L Westley, a native of Northwood, Blair County, paid the ultimate price for his country during World War II.

Donald was born on April 23, 1918, the second youngest of ten children, which included seven brothers and three sisters. Five of the brothers served in World War II.

In 1940, Westley enlisted with Troop B, 104th Calvary, Pennsylvania National Guard and trained at Fort Indiantown Gap. His troop was called into service in February 1941. Then, he also served at Fort Bragg, North Carolina; Fort Pendleton, Oregon; and Ford Ord, California.

After basic training, Westley was sent to serve in the Aleutian Islands, just off of Alaska, where he spent seven months fighting the Japanese. He later returned to Camp Maxey, Texas in December 1943. After a brief furlough home, Westley received orders sending him to the European Theater of Operations, where he served in France, Luxembourg, and Belgium.

CPL Westley was injured in The Battle of the Bulge in Belgium on Dec 27, 1944 and succumbed to those injuries on December 30, 1944.

According to Westley's nephew, also named Don Westley, CPL Westley's older brother Oren Ambrose Westley (the younger Don's father) was stationed in the same area as his brother.

Oren visited the Henri Chapelle American Military Cemetery in Henri Chapelle, Belgium and put flowers at the grave at the cross. He took pictures and sent them home to his dad. Westley was buried in that cemetery from 1944-47. Then in 1947, he was moved to Tyrone, where he laid in state at the EUB church. The American Legion Honor Guard stood guard over him. After the services, he was then buried at the Eastlawn Cemetery.

For his service, CPL Westley was posthumously awarded the Purple Heart, World War II Victory Medal, and the Honorable Service Lapel Button.

The younger Westley says that a few years ago, he and

two other relatives were cleaning out the family homestead, where CPL Westley's younger brother had lived, and found this information regarding the Corporal. They decided to go to Jim Gregory's office to find out about the possibility of having a local bridge in Tyrone named after their uncle.

They were told to bring all of the information that they had on him to the office and they would see what they could do. They checked on whether or not the specific bridge that they were thinking about would be able to be renamed. All of this took place in 2019. According to the younger Westley, it took a good while for the entire process. First, it went through the House of Representatives and passed and then it went to the Pennsylvania State Senate where it passed.

The bridge is located at State Route 4027 over The Bald Eagle Creek, near the paper mill. According to the younger Westley, his uncle was born and raised about a half a mile from the bridge. "How many times he may have crossed that bridge during his young life is hard to tell," Westley questions.

About fifty to seventy-five people, mostly relatives, attended the bridge ceremony along with Jim Gregory and Judy Ward as well as representatives from Tyrone and John Joyce's office.

The Westley family would like to thank all veterans who served and all military personnel who are currently serving and training to keep America safe and free.

**Information for this article was obtained through a phone interview with Don Westley
**Photos were provided by Don Westley

DON WITHERSPOON

DON WITHERSPOON

For longtime president of the Blair County chapter of the NAACP Don Witherspoon, human rights wasn't about color.

Witherspoon's vice-president, Bill Sweet, said that Witherspoon would advocate for civil and human rights. "We would visit prisons and answer complaints from the prisoners. If they needed representation, we would sit down with them and listen to what they had to say. We visited every prison within a six-county area at one time or another," Sweet said. The two would also address complaints of discrimination in the workplace.

Sweet says that, with Don, it wasn't the matter of race. Witherspoon's nephew, Jeremiah Witherspoon Jr, agreed. "Witherspoon helped thousands of individuals," Jeremiah said. Witherspoon gave scholarships out to young athletes. He treated people the way that he wanted to be treated. He worked for equality for all people, Jeremiah said.

Pennsylvania state Rep. Jim Gregory (R-80th) was a friend of Witherspoon's. Gregory said that he was first introduced to Witherspoon and his character when he accompanied PA state Sen. Robert Jubelirer to an NAACP dinner. Gregory said that Witherspoon loved that dinner, which was his project. Witherspoon put "everything he had into it," Gregory said.

"Just watching him in the room at The Calvin House with all of the luminaries. All walks of life in the room. He was just like a king among us. Even our own Martin Luther King in Blair County, but also a king among everyone," Gregory continued.

Witherspoon was one of those folks who didn't take himself too seriously. He enjoyed what he was doing and worked hard at it. Even so, many times, Gregory said, there was a visible weight on his shoulders. "The people who he was representing, speaking on behalf of and trying to help—it could be a lot. It could just be a lot," Gregory said.

Gregory realized that, as an elected official, he needed guidance following the killing of George Floyd of Minneapolis on May 25, 2020. Witherspoon recognized that there was a need to be "proactive". What needed to be done as an elected official was to have sensitivity to the issue. Gregory said that there was only one person who he could call. Witherspoon told him, "Jim, be yourself. You have always been supportive of the black community. Just be there for them." Gregory said being able to have Witherspoon as a resource meant "so much."

Witherspoon, who became president of the NAACP in the 80's, made a lot of changes for the area as far as justice and equality. He always looked at things from both angles and then came to the conclusion about what needed to be done.

Sweet remembers, "With Don's personality, he could get along with everybody. It wasn't the matter of your race. He had this ability to sit people down and get things done." He adds, "When you thought of the NAACP, you thought of Don Witherspoon, because he put his entire life into it— 24/7."

Gregory recalls an awesome moment on the golf course with Witherspoon. "Don was legendary when it came to his love of golf. I golfed with him many many times. One of our greatest memories was being part of a foursome at Iron Masters for The Chamber of Commerce Golf outing. I hit the drive on number eight. We were about 130 yards out and Don hit the second shot and put it in the hole for an eagle on what is one of the toughest holes in Blair County." Gregory says that to have that as a memory to chuckle about..."When you golf with someone, it shows their character. Golf is a game of gentlemen. He was a true gentleman on the golf course and in life."

Jeremiah said that Witherspoon was "very genuine". He said that he would look out for people and he would check up on those who were in the hospital.

"He just made everybody feel like he cared about them." Gregory said.

Jeremiah adds, "We just need to pick up where he left off and run with it. Always make change."

Witherspoon passed away December of 2020.

**Portions of this article was originally written by the author for the Morrison Cove Herald in December 2020
**Information for this interview was obtained through phone interviews with Bill Sweet, Jeremiah Witherspoon and Pennsylvania State Representative Jim Gregory
**Photos were provided by Linda Witherspoon

CHARLES E. WOLF

Founder: Charles E. Wolf
Born: October 28, 1864
Died: October 18, 1918

Charles E. Wolf

THE WOLF FAMILY

Though the beginning of Wolf Furniture is officially considered to be 1902, it was not the family's first venture into business. They can trace their business roots back to the mid to late 1800s.

Adam J. Wolf, who settled in Hollidaysburg, was in the cabinet making and undertaking business. In 1843, at the age of twenty-two, he crossed the Atlantic and after residing two years in Philadelphia, he moved to Hollidaysburg and worked as a journeyman cabinet maker. Shortly, thereafter, he started in business for himself. He built cabinet making and undertaking rooms on Allegheny Street.

Former company president, Doug Wolf, says back in those days, there wasn't a place that you would go to buy a casket. It had to be made usually by the undertaker. When they didn't have a client people would ask, "Can you make a table or chairs?" After being in the furniture business and undertaking business for a number of years, Adam transferred the business to his eldest son, William.

Adam and his wife had a family of six sons. There was William, who took over his father's business; Henry A, who was a partner in the Altoona Hardware and Supply Company; Salem Joseph, who was also in the hardware business; Adam Richard, also a hardware dealer; Charles E, a hardware dealer and eventual founder of Wolf Furniture; and Frank X who died at the age of sixteen.

Charles Eugene Wolf, born October 28, 1864, in Hollidaysburg, opened several flourishing businesses in Pennsylvania and Ohio and invested so carefully and wisely that he retired when he was forty years old.

About 1885, while Charles was working in A.J. Wolf Hardware Store in Hollidaysburg, a traveling salesman brought news of an oil boom in Lima, Ohio. Charles bought a bankrupt hardware store and operated the Wolf Hardware Store in Lima for several years. The oil boom died out in the late eighties or early nineties. Then, Charles returned east, and the C.E. Wolf Hardware Company became the next venture at 1414 Eleventh Avenue in Altoona.

It is presumed that the C.E. Wolf Hardware Company was sold to Salem J. Wolf because he operated a hardware store at the same location for many years before moving to 1712 Eleventh Avenue. Charles was manager of the Altoona Equipment Company, which was later known as the Standard Supply and Equipment Company until March 1, 1902.

Also, in the 1890s, Charles E Wolf, Albert J Anderson, A.R. Wolf, and perhaps others, incorporated the Union Furnace Manufacturing Company—a corporation formed to manufacture shovels at a mill at Union Furnace in Huntingdon County, Pennsylvania.

Also, using his savings and credit, he had purchased 1313 Eleventh Avenue, Altoona and with John A Fox and Charles M. Fox had started Fox and Fox, the first of what he intended to be a chain of novelty stores. John Fox was manager and Charles Wolf acted as a silent partner. This arrangement continued until 1902 when John A Fox sold his share to the other two partners, probably to get enough money in 1902 to buy his share in the newly formed City Furniture Company. C.E. Wolf had much to do with the combining of two local electric light companies; the Edison Electric and Illuminating Company and the Citizens Electric Light Company.

In 1896, Quandt and Cherry, merchant tailors at 1427 Eleventh Avenue, had built a four-story brick business block at 901-903 Green Avenue for Harry Wayne to conduct a retail furniture business. Wayne had not made a success of it, and by 1902 Charles heard that Wayne had wanted to get out of the business. He authorized John Fox to make the deal with Quandt and Cherry and Wayne. They wanted $14,280 for the business. Fox was to put up $5,000. Charles was to put up $10,000 in stock of the Union Furnace Manufacturing Company by May 15, 1902.

Formally, the family recognizes 1902, with the establishment of City Furniture, as the beginning of their furniture business.

Over the years, Charles Wolf made it a rule not to buy or to speculate in residential property, but he was always interested in buying and trading Eleventh Avenue business properties, generally at a greater or lesser profit, because Altoona was growing, and chain stores were starting to come in. At one time, Charles had dreams of a chain of ten-cent stores and as a number two store, he started The Imperial Novelty Company on Third Street in Harrisburg. No more stores were opened, possibly due to the buying of the City Furniture Company. The Imperial Novelty Company was liquidated about 1913.

Charles had five children, all born at home: George Anderson Wolf, John Joseph Wolf, Herbert Thomas Wolf, Margaret Elizabeth and Dorothy Seton Wolf. The three boys all worked in the store. Charles managed the store. George A handled the office, credits, and some advertising. John did part of the buying and selling, Herb was in charge of credit and in addition did a full day's work on the outside collecting, selling and like all other employees worked on Saturday evenings.

C.E.W. was vice-president of the Altoona Baseball Club during the years it was in the Tri-State League. He, also, owned stock in the Altoona Times as well as The Mountain City Trust Company.

In 1911, the corner of Eleventh Avenue and 15th Street with a frontage of 43 feet was for sale. In addition, the block back of the corner could be bought—that is, the corner of Tenth Avenue and 15th Street. After extensive negotiations, Charles personally bought the parcels for $40,000. It was a splendid plot for a furniture store with extra width on Tenth Avenue for stables. Horses were used to pull delivery wagons in those days.

Soon the name change came from City Furniture company to Wolf's City Furniture Company and then just Wolf Furniture Company.

During September 1918, the influenza epidemic returned and about October 10, 1918, Charles E. Wolf picked up the germ and on October 18, 1918, he died

"During bad times, lots of customers owed the company money. The company knew our customers didn't have any money, so trying to collect was not going to be effective and not viewed well. So, the company was very benevolent in those days about giving people flexible terms that created a lot of good will when the country came out of The Depression. The employees kept their jobs, and the customers didn't have to get their furniture repossessed and they were still able to buy. That was a key period."

During the depression years, they took payments in coal, eggs, and vegetables. In this way, Wolf's earned customer trust and support. The business grew and developed. It survived the depression of 1929-1937.

The Wolfs, then remodeled the Altoona store. When completed, the firm utilized all six floors, giving the store a sales and display floor space of 63,450 square feet, the largest in the section of the state devoted to the marketing of home furnishings.

In 1948, George A. And Herbert T. established the Wolf Fund. The proceeds under the initial grant were to be used to improve the city industrially, recreationally, socially, and civically. In 1948, the initial grant was $10,000, and the fund purposes stated that this fund will be spent for the betterment of Altoona and its citizens.

Both George and Herbert were generous to the Catholic High School. At one time, they purchased all the property from 1101 to 1111 on Seventh Avenue and donated it to the school.

George A Wolf

During the "Jobs for Joes" Campaign in Altoona, Wolf's kicked off the drive with a donation of $20,000. Doug adds, "One of the hallmarks of our business was that we were community and charity focused. We believed that we were part of the community where our employees lived and worked."

Doug continues, "In Altoona, over the years, gifts were made to schools and the arts such as Penn State Altoona, St Francis University, Bishop Guilfoyle High School, The Southern Alleghenies Museum of Art, BCAF and dozens of local charities and youth sports every year. It was part of the fabric and culture of the family and the company." That philanthropy continues through the Wolf/Kuhn Foundation which gives out in excess of $100,000 annually to Blair County Arts and Education Charities.

G.A. Wolf served as president of Wolf's from 1918 until his retirement in 1965 and was an active member of the Altoona business community during these years. With his brother Herbert T. Wolf Sr, he expanded the company from the original store in Altoona to a chain of stores within a 100-mile radius of Altoona. George went along with Herb on the expansion program, but only on the condition that each store stand on its own two feet with little help from the anchor Altoona store.

G.A. was a charter member of and past president of the Altoona Kiwanis Club. As a member of the Blair County Historical Society, he had a keen interest in local history. He liked history and personally took it upon himself the task of editor of the book Blair County: The First Hundred Years, 1846-1946.

G.A. Wolf hoped to see the family carry on the furniture

business through his eldest son, George A Wolf Jr, however, he was killed aboard the U.S.S. Arizona at Pearl Harbor on December 7, 1941. His third son, Gerald Prendergast Wolf was able and willing to carry on the family tradition of the Wolf Furniture Company.

Herbert Thomas Wolf had the following children: Peggy, Sally, Herb Jr, and John. Herb Jr and John continued the family tradition in the carrying on of The Wolf Furniture Company.

Herbert T. Wolf

After over a hundred years, Wolf Furniture moved its corporate headquarters and distribution center to Bellwood in the early 2000s.

Over the years, Wolf's had stores in Virginia, West Virginia, Maryland, and Pennsylvania. "We had as many as twenty-nine at one time."

In thinking about what enabled the company to last over 100 years, Doug says that he would have to say that "It was our stable ownership and quality employees. If we took care of our employees, our employees would take care of our customers." He continues, "In turn, the customers were loyal to them and the company. It sounds trite, but it was a practice which proved to be very successful, weathering the many, economic ups and downs."

Doug talks about how being a Blair County based business helped them throughout the years. "I would say that Blair County is special. It is a wonderful place to live, a wonderful place to raise a family, a wonderful place to be raised and it was a stable environment to have our company based. There wasn't a lot of turn over. There wasn't a lot of peaks and valleys to economic cycles in this area. That allowed us to be a stable player offering a century of continued service to our customers in a pretty wide geography.

"Being based out of Blair County for all of those years, we were still ranked in the top 100 furniture retailers in the United States. For probably the last thirty or forty years, even though our population was low, we were able to do a lot of business out of this area. We were able to retain high quality employees because there was a good quality of life. It wasn't a large urban rat race with tons of turnover and things that affect longevity in a business. We found Blair County to be a terrific place to be headquartered and if you look around here, there have been many businesses, which have terrific national, regional, or mid-Atlantic success. There are hidden gems all through our area and you can learn from what they have done. It is not just possible, it happens."

Doug recalls, "We prided ourselves in our business on having employee seniority. The company was sold in 2017, to one of the largest furniture companies in the country and they failed. That's tragic and probably one of the differences was that they did not foster and maintain a relationship with their employees. You can't run a good business without good employees."

Doug says that the reason that they decided to sell was that several key executives were approaching retirement age and there was no active family interested in maintaining the business. They had what looked like a great opportunity for their employees to be joined up with one of the best furniture guys in the entire industry. He adds, "It is heartbreaking to see how it failed."

The legacy that Doug hopes the company leaves is one of doing business with Blair County families for several generations. "We were chosen, trusted and served family after family for multiple generations. Not a lot of businesses can say that."

Many Wolf family members retain ownership in Wolf Realty Associates; A family run realty company operating in Pennsylvania, Maryland, and West Virginia, along with other independent family business endeavors.

It was once said of Charles E. Wolf, "He was a fine man to do business with and to work for and must have handed it down to his sons these same qualities which account for your success."

Doug said, "We have a deep and lasting respect and admiration for the people of Blair County on the first frontier."

** Information for this article was obtained through the following resources:
1. Phone Interview with Doug Wolf
2. The Wolf Furniture Company From 1902-1970 by Wallace A Riley
3. Biography: Charles E. Wolf (1864-1918), Founder Wolf Furniture Company

**Photos were obtained from Doug Wolf and from The Wolf Furniture Company From 1902-1970 by Wallace A Riley.

FINAL WORDS....FOR NOW

All of these great people are just a small portion of those who have achieved notable accomplishments in their personal and/or professional lives. The following is a list of more people from Blair County, some of which you may be reading about in additional editions of this series.

If you know of someone who you believe should be on this list, please submit your suggestions by visiting our website at www.theycamefrompa.com and be on the lookout for future editions of this book series.

NOTABLE PEOPLE FROM BLAIR COUNTY

- Abe Ajay - Artist

- Jacob Ake-Founder of Williamsburg

- John Ake - Baseball Player

- Randy Allen - Basketball Player

- Michael Allison-Artist

- John Anastasi MD - Playwright

- Jared Angle - Actor

- Tyler Angle - Dancer

- Harry J Anslinger - 1st Commissioner of The Federal Bureau of Narcotics

- Christian Appleman - College Tennis

- Don Appleman - High School Basketball

- Erin Appleman - College Volleyball

- Jeff Appleman - High School Basketball Coach

- Elaini Arthur - singer

- Steve Aungst - Singer, Music Promoter/Agent, Founder of The Vicksburg Quartet, Pennsylvania Southern Gospel Music Association HOF

- Elias Baker - Owned Allegheny Furnace

- Mary Baker - High School Coach

- Mary Replogle Baker - Javelin

- Judge Thomas Baldridge - Pennsylvania Attorney General and Pennsylvania Superior Court Judge

- Daniel M Bare Jr. - Founder of The Roaring Spring Paper Mill and Roaring Spring Blank Book

- Arlan Barkman - Pro Baseball

- Billy Baron - Basketball Player

- Addison Basenback - American Ninja Warrior Jr Contestant

- Dale Batzel - High School Coach

- Candi White Beatty - Appeared in Ladies Home Journal with Michelle Obama as a Single mother female veteran

- Donny Beaver - Entrepreneur

- Leonard Beerman - Rabbi

- Louis and Michael Beezer - (aka The Beezer Brothers) - Architects

- Michael Behe - Biochemist, Author and Intelligent Design Advocate

- Thomas Behe - Engineer/Scientist and Inventor

- Jacob Belinda - Baseball Player

- Charles Alvin Bell - Actor

- Edward "Neddy" Bell - Founded Bellwood, Owned Elizabeth Furnace

- Martin Bell - devised a system of using escaping gasses from the iron furnace to give added power to the operation and secured a patent for the process

- Brad Benson - Football Player

- Troy Benson - Football Player

- Marisa Bertani - Actress

- Andrew Jackson Bettwy - Politician

- Steve Betza - Corporate Director for Lockheed Martin

- Michael Biddle - Javelin

- Dina Bilofsky - Dancer

- Jennifer Black Reinhardt - Children's Illustrator

- Jeremiah S Black - State Supreme Court Judge

- Dr. Maureen Black - Pediatric Pshychologist

- Black Coffee Productions - (consisting of Eli Austin, Nathan Larimer and Josh Rimmey) - Video Production

- Janet Blair - Actress

- Arthur Blake - Actor

- Ron Blazier - Baseball Player

- Jeanne Bolger - Singer/Entertainer

- Charles Bonebreak - High School Coach

- Rob Boston - Director of Communications for Americans United for Separation of church and state

- Jeff Bower - Basketball General Manager

- Danah Boyd - Social Media Scholar

- Tim Boyles - Celebrity Photographer

- Gregg Brandt - Actor and Singer

- Paul Revere Braniff - Airline Entrepeneur

- Charlie Brenneman - Mixed Martial Artist

- Christian Bridenbaugh - Pro Baseball

- Philip H Bridenbaugh - Football Player and Coach

- Samuel Held Bridenbaugh - Clergy

- Robert Broadwater - Author

- Steven J. Brown - Cinematograper

- D. Emmert Brumbaugh - US Congressman

- John Brumbaugh - Pro Baseball

- John Buchanan-Leading Presbyterian Editor/ Publisher of The Christian Century

- Richard Buckley - High School Basketball Coach

- Elmer Burket - Photographer

- Lowell Burket - Discovered Hybrid Bird (Burket's Warbler)

- Bucky Bush - Baseball Player

- Edward and Rose Byers - Established Morrisons Cove High School

- Samuel Calvin - US Congressman 1848-1851

- Crystal Cameron - Christian Singer

- Willard Campbell - Entrepreneur (Founder of Hoss's)

- Bill Campion - Basketball Player

- Samuel Canan - Military and Politician

- Susan Candiotti - Journalist

- Andrew Carnegie - Steel Magnate - Lived in Altoona

- John A Casciotti - US Department of Defense

- Bill Casper - High School Basketball Coach

- Edward B Cassatt - Owner/Breeder of Thorough-bred Horses

- Mary Cassatt - Artist

- Patrick Cassidy - Founded Newry Borough

- John Castle - Spartan World Championships

- Tech Sgt John A Chapman - Medal of Honor Recipient

- Dr Robert Charles - MIT Graduate and Researcher

- Marcella Cisney - Actress

- Jim and Jane Claar - Country Music Duo

- Matt Claar-C-SPAN

- Harry Clarke - High School Coach

- Melinda Clarke - Peace Activist

- Terry Clarke - Barbershop Quartet International Champion 1980

- Sam Cohn - Talent Agent

- Henry Colman - TV Writer/ Producer

- Ripper Collins - Baseball Player

- Dick Conlon - Boxer

- Frank Conrad-Father of Radio Broadcasting

- Robert C Cook-Founded software company "Systems Inc"

- Mark Whitey Cooper - Actor and Musician

- Tom Corbo - Football Player

- Kristin Cougar-Dancer

- Frederick Counsel-Painter

- Denny Cowher - Semi-Pro Baseball, Bedford County Sports HOF, Pennsylvania American Legion Hall of Fame

- Robert Edward Cox-Medal of Honor Recipient

- Thomas C Creighton - Politician

- Stan Crilly-Artist/Photographer

- Charlie Crist - Politician

- Jim Curry - Football Player

- Angela Dodson Daeger-Singer, Entertainment Executive

- Carole D'Andrea - Actress

- David DeArmond - U.S. Congressman

- Gene Decker-Semi-Pro Baseball Hall of Fame

- Robert Glen Decker - Actor

- Kayla DeCriscio-College Basketball Player

- DelGrosso Family - DelGrosso Foods and Amusement Park

- Sharon Sager Desch - Engineer

- Lino Diaz - Baseball Player and Coach

- Charles Dickson - Dancer

- Karly Diebold - Fourth Place in National FFA Agriscience Fair

- Paul C Donnelly - NASA

- Gordon Dooley - Actor

- James Dugan - Historian, Author and screenwriter

- Samuel Duncan - Founder of Duncansville

- Jon Eardley - Jazz Trumpeter

- Blaine Earon - Football Player

- John Ebersole - Football Player

- Orville Ebersole - Big Game Hunter

- Helen Eby-Rock - Actress

- Scott Edmiston - Theater and Educator

- Josh Eggebeen - Film Industry

- John Eichelberger - Politician

- Keith England - Actor

- Glenn H. English Jr - Medal of Honor Recipient

- Barry Ernest - JFK Assassination Expert

- Jim Fall - TV and Movie Director

- Kenneth Ferry - Founder of WJSM Radio

- Nick Finochio - Photographer

- Ron Fiochetta - AAABA Hall of Fame

- Leonard S Fiore - Construction and Real Estate

- Ed Flanagan - Football Player

- Kaleb Fleck - Baseball Player

- Samuel B. Fluke - Photographer

- Danny Fortson - Basketball Player

- Rebecca Foust - Poet/Writer

- George Fox - Four Chaplains-USS Dorchester WWII - raised in Altoona

- Brian Franco - Football Player

- Jared Frederick - Historian and guest host on Turner Classic Movies

- John Frederick - Bicyclist, Author

- Jason Freehling - Actor

- Jacob Karl Fries - Architect

- Donald Fuoss - Football And Basketball coach

- Candace Futrell - Basketball Player

- William F Gable—Founder Gables Department Store

- H.B. Galbraith - Football Coach

- Karen Gallagher - Tennis Player

- Frank Gansz - Football Coach

- Christian Garber - Pennsylvania Senator and Congressman

- James "Pike" Gardner - Founder of Gardner's Candy

- Russell Garver - Co-Founder of Roaring Spring

- Brian Gates - Martial Artist, Stunt Man, and Bodyguard

- Dean Gates - Pro Baseball

- Lisa Gehret - Basketball Player

- Wayne "Buddy" Geis - Football Coach

- Richard Geist - Politician

- Honorary Robert Gibson - Baseball Player, Federal Judge

- Aaron Gilbert - Artist

- Angie Gioiosa - Long Distance Running

- Joseph A Giovinazzo (stage name of Frank DeSal) - Actor, Dancer and Director

- Kevin Givens - Football Player

- Fred Glasgow - Fighter Pilot

- Chris Glass - Semi-Pro Baseball Hall of Fame

- John Gochnaur - Baseball Player

- Jaysen Gold - Singer

- Martin Goldberg - Tennis

- Shirley Goldfarb - Painter and writer

- Bob Gordon - Pro Baseball

- Shawn Gority - Irish Folk Musician

- Gospel Sounds Duet - Christian Singers

- Jim Gregory - Media Personality and Politician

- Galen Hall - Football Coach

- Willard Lee Hall - Actor

- Brian Hallinan - Boxer

- Hugh Halpern - Recipient of The John W McCormick Award of Excellence

- Hugh Halpern - Director of the Government Publishing Office

- Harry R Harr - WWII Congressional Medal of Honor

- Caitlin Harshberger - National Inspiring Teen Magazine All - star Cheerleader

- Steve Hatfield - Football Player

- John Hayes - Pennsylvania State Football Coaches Association Hall of Fame

- Samuel E. Hayes Jr - Pennsylvania Congressman

- Tom Healy - Baseball Player

- Frederick Heck - Actor

- Autumn Helsel - High School Basketball
- Hope Hibbard - Biologist, Cytologist, zoologist and professor of zoology
- John S Hickman - Civil War Congressional Medal of Honor Recipient
- Josiah Duane Hicks - Politician
- Col. Jacob Higgins - Military
- Bernard E. Hinish - Pro Baseball
- Dave Hoenstine - Baseball Player
- Lynn Hoffner - Pro Baseball
- Andrea Lee Hollen - First Female Graduate of West Point
- Jared Hollingshead - Model
- Bryan Holly - Actor
- Doug Hoover - Biathalon Champion
- Brian A Hopkins - Writer
- Hedda Hopper - Gossip Columnist and Actress
- Vaugn Horton - Songwriter HOF
- Avery Howsare - Football Player
- Julian Howsare - Football Player
- Abby Hoy - High School Basketball
- Adam Huber - Actor
- Dennie Huber - Entertainer

- Ashely Hughes - Former Child Actress

- Robert C Hunt - Painter

- Maxwell Hunter - Aerospace Engineer

- Harold L. Ickes - Politician

- Fredina Iffert – Racquetball Player

- Fred Imler Sr and The Imler Family - Imler's Poultry

- Mike Irwin - Football Player

- Pat Irwin - Volunteer for Mother's Merry Children's Center

- Tom Irwin Jr - Bishop Guilfoyle Football Coach

- Tommy Irwin - Baseball Player

- Mike Iuzzolino - Basketball Player

- William Jack - Financial Investor, Industrialist

- Edwin A Jaggard - Jurist

- Betty James - Business Person

- Richard T James - Inventor

- Major General Vernon James - Military

- TJ Jefferson - TV Producer and Production Manager

- Jerek - Actor

- Erin Johnson - High School Basketball, Featured in Sports Illustrated

- Stan Jones - Football Player

- John Joyce - Politician

- Robert Jubelirer - Politician

- Theodore H Kattouf - Diplomat

- Courtney Kaup - Triathlete

- Chester Keefer - Physician (Penicilin Czar)

- Denny Kelly - Actor, Film Production

- Michele Winkler Kennedy - Helped decorate The White House for Christmas 2017

- George E. Kensinger - Pro Baseball, PIAA Basketball Offiicial

- Dave Kerr Jr. - Beagling Hall of Fame

- Donn Kinzle - Olympic Track Coach

- Brittany Kleiner - Reality Show contestant

- Henry Kloss - Audio Engineer and Entrepeneur

- Otto Kneidinger - Football Player and Coach

- Bill Koontz - Sea Farer transporting animals from America to Poland

- Michael Koorman - Composer

- Honorary Jolene Kopriva - First Female Judge in Blair County

- Lionel Krantz - Playwright

- Kenneth M Kuhn - Painter/ Jazz Drummer

- Jason Kuntz - Wrestling Coach

- Jacob Banks Kurtz - Politician
- Laura Kustaborder - Mountain Climber
- Steve Lach - Football Player
- Sam Lafferty - Hockey Player
- Dylan Lane - TV Game Show host
- Vaughn O Lang - LT General in US Army
- Fred J. Lauver - Author and Actor
- Robert E Laws - Medal of Honor Recipient
- Thomas Leamer - College President
- Ricky Lee - Singer
- Denny Lingenfelter - Baseball Player
- John Lingenfelter - Race Car Driver
- Walter Lingenfelter - Big Game Hunter
- Brian, Greg and Terry Long – Winners of Junkyard Wars
- Jeffrey Long - Construction and Real Estate
- Eldin Lower - High School Baseball, Basketball and Football
- Marion Lower - Military, Attorney
- James Loy - US Secretary of Homeland Security
- Bob and Joan Lozinak - Owners of the Altoona Curve
- Michael Luckett - Baseball Player

- Chad Luensmann - Baseball Player

- Primo Lusardi - POW

- Stephanie Lytle - TV and Movie Production Assistant

- Dean Maddox - Musician and Tamburitzan

- James Madera - CEO of American Medical Association

- Ronald Mallett - Theoretical Physicist, Academic and Author

- Eric Malone - Watercraft Sports Pioneer

- Pat Malone - Baseball

- Marvin Mangus - Geologist and Landscape Painter

- William Abram Mann - Military

- Anthony Mannino - Actor

- Joe Martin - Baseball Player

- Steve Mason - Broadcaster

- Wallace McCamant - Jurist

- Jon McClintock - TV reporter, Actor and Congressional Press Secretary

- Ray McDonald - Received the Purple Heart

- Bob McDonogh - Racecar Driver

- Dean McGee - PA Football HOF, PIAA Official for Basketball, Baseball and Football

- Bob McGregor - Golfer, Model

- John J McGuire - Sci-Fi Author

- Tim McKelvey - Emmy Award for Outstanding Period Costume

- J. King McLanahan - Industrialist and Inventor

- Ward McLanahan - Olympian

- Matthew McLoota - TV and Movie Production

- Tiffani McNeilis - Wrestler

- The Meadows Family - Meadows Family Custard

- Gene "Pappy" Merritts - Nashville Swing Musician

- Jim Merritts - Football Player

- Kevin Metrocavage - International Space Station Operations Manager

- Curtis Miller - Basketball Player

- Reid Miller - Football Player

- Grace Misera - Actress

- Hannah Misera - Actress

- Johnny Moore - Basketball Player

- John Moorehead Jr - Golfer

- Brian Morden - Actor

- Chris Morrison - Actor

- Susan Wise Moses and Jacob Moses - Parents of Annie Oakley

- Jimmy Mowery - Singer and Voice Contestant

- C Stowe Myers - Industrial Designer

- William Myers - Actor

- Annette Nagle - Educator (Teaches students in China online)

- George N Nagle - 2012 Presidential Candidate

- Herman R Nagle - Author and Historian

- Danny Napoleon - Baseball Player

- W. Albert Nason - Founded Nason Hospital

- AJ Nastasi - High School Basketball

- Joe Nastasi Jr. - Pro Football

- Pauline Neff - Actress

- William Nesbit - Civil Rights Leader

- Jeff Neuman - Basketball Player

- Julie Nevel - Author and Singer

- Ron Noel - International Businessman

- Richard E Nugent - Military

- Leo J (Lee) O'Connor - Drummer

- Dan Ott - Poker Player

- Betsy Padamonsky - Actress and singer

- Jackie Paisley - Female Bodybuilder

- Helen (Camp) Palmer - War Correspondent

- Mark Panek - Drummer

- Bill Parsons - Tennis Player
- Maury Patt - Football Player
- Dave Patterson - Marathon Runner
- George Patterson - Pennsylvania Congressman
- Marion Patterson - Pennsylvania State Supreme Court
- Georgina Pazcoguin - Ballet Dancer
- John Pielmeier - Author and Playwright
- Mandi Pierce - College Basketball Coach
- H Beam Piper - Sci-Fi Author
- Eugene Smokey Pleacher - Country Singer/ Musician
- Ashley Pletcher - Horse Trick Rider
- Matt Plowman - YouTube Personality
- Rena Popp - TV News Producer
- Joe Port - TV Writer and Producer
- Moses Port – TV Writer and Producer
- Fish Pote - Artist
- Duggie Potter - Singer
- Ray Prosperi - Football Player
- Steve Prosser - Musician
- Brent Pry - Football Player and Coach
- Patricia Pyuen - Actress

- Kelly M Quintanilla - Academic

- Bob Ramazzotti - Baseball Player

- Mark Raugh - Football Player

- Samuel Rea - President of the PRR

- Matthew Reed - Actor

- Nunzio Rehm - Price is Right Contestant

- Mike Reid - Singer and Football Player

- John Reilly - Politician

- Kent Replogle - National Television Educator and Executive

- Luther I Replogle - Nominated by Nixon to be ambassador to Ireland

- Jim Restauri - Boxer

- Luke Rhodes - Football Player

- Renee Riccio McCutchan - Swimmer

- Dick Rice - Motorcycle excursion along The Oregon Trail

- Hap Ritchey - WVAM, WJSM, Pennsylvania Southern gospel Music Association HOF

- Oliver Ritchey - Founder of Ritchey's Dairy

- Charles M Robinson - Architect

- Mike Rose - Educator

- Austin Rosenberry - Football Player

- Jackie Russo - Pageant Director

- Typhani Russo - Model

- Emme Rylan - Actress

- Steve Saive - Musician

- Bob Savine - Jazz Drummer

- Wade Schalles - Wrestler

- Tawney Nardozza Schmitt - Swimmer

- Dr Peter Schoenberger - Iron Master

- Charles M Schwab - Steel Magnate

- Eric Sciotto - Actor

- Cecil Harmon Scott - WWII Ball Gunner Memphis Belle

- Thomas Scott - President of the PRR

- Jack Servello - Singer/Musician

- Joe Servello - Illustrator/Artist

- Susan Severson - Painter

- Erika Shay - Casting Director

- Scott Sheehan - Grammy Nominated Music Teacher

- Sheetz Family - Entrepreneurs

- Steven Sherrill - Writer/Poet

- Sara E Skrabalak - Academic

- Tracey Slogik - Basketball Player

- Smith Cobras - Softball Team that won The World Amateur Softball Association Class A Championship in 1988

- D Brooks Smith - US Court of Appeals Judge

- Denver "Junie" Smith - Decathalon

- George "Germany" Smith - Baseball Player

- Larry Smith - Author and Historian

- Margaret "Peg" Augusta McCartney Smith - Writer/Poet

- Jake Snyder - Singer/Musician

- D Raymond Sollenberger - Pennsylvania Congressman

- Harry Edward Soyster - Military

- Jerry Stern - Pennsylvania Congressman

- Lynn Stewart - Country Singer

- Ethan Stiefel - Dancer and Choreographer

- Frederick Martin "Baldy" Stoehr - Baseball Player

- John A Stormer - Author

- Frank R. Strayer - Movie Director

- Earl Strohm - Football Coach

- Wilmer Stultz - Aviator

- Don Swanson - Cinematographer

- Tom Sweitzer - Playwright

- Heather Taddy - Paranormal Researcher/TV Personality

- Art Taneyhill - Nationally recognized High School Basketball Coach

- Steve Taneyhill - Football Player

- Jill Tate - High Scholl Basketball

- Charles (Chuck) Taylor - Boxer

- Harry Temple - Football Player

- Allyson Tessin - Geologist/Oceanographer

- Brian Tychinski - Band Director (part of The London New Years Day Parade 2020

- James E. Van Zandt - Politician

- Andrew Kevin Walker - Screenwriter

- Walkney - Singer

- Tina Marie Walter - Singer

- Jacob Walters – Founder of Walterstown, which eventually became part of Duncansville

- William B Walton - Politician

- Fred Waring - Musician and Big Band Leader

- Jennifer Lynn Warren - Actress

- Rebecca Nori Wattenschaidt - Social Media Influencer/ Business Person

- Jake Webb - Boxer

- Doug West – Basketball Player

- Army CPL Donald L. Westley - Military/Purple Heart Recipient

- Kenneth Weyant - Big Game Hunter

- Mindy Weyer - Dancer

- Red Whitaker - Roboticist

- Coredelia White - First Female School Teacher in Altoona

- Daniel Hale Williams - African American General Surgeon

- George C Wilson - Entrepreneur

- Dr James Thompson Wilson - Physician, Inventor

- Dennis Wilt - Educator

- Tom Wilt - Boxer

- Paul Winter - Saxophonist

- Alfie Wise - Actor

- Don Witherspoon - NAACP President

- Aline Wolf - Writer and Leading Thinker on Education Methods

- Charles E. Wolf and The Wolf Family - Wolf Furniture

- Jim Worthing - Singer with The Cumberland Boys at The Grand Ole Opry

- Len Zandy - Basketball and Baseball Player

- Shawn Zimmerman - Professional Bull Rider

- Edwin Zoller - Painter

- Jeff Zona - Pro Baseball

AUTHOR BIOGRAPHY

Author Eric Shields is a Blair County native and currently calls Altoona, Pennsylvania home. He is a fan of local history and of those who have helped to create it by using their knowledge and skills in their respective areas of expertise.

He is a part-time community theatre actor with Off Pitt Street Theatre in Bedford, PA, The Claysburg Community Theatre in Claysburg, PA, and Cove Community Theater in Loysburg, PA. He has also appeared in the Altoona shot short film No Game Like Foxes (2020), the award-winning Pittsburgh shot Mulligan (2018) and music video Blinds featuring Matt Otis and the Sound.

Shields is excited about the release of his second edition

of *They Came From Blair County* and is looking forward to the release of future editions of the Blair County portion of the *They Came From PA* series. Shields also looks forward to expanding the series into other areas of Central and Western Pennsylvania including *They Came From Bedford County* and *They Came From Cambria County*.

To learn more about the book series, please visit our website www.theycamefrompa.com or any of our current Facebook pages, *They Came From Blair County, They Came From Bedford County, They Came From Cambria County,* and *They Came From Pittsburgh.*

CPSIA information can be obtained
at www.ICGtesting.com
Printed in the USA
BVHW050935250522
638036BV00016B/313